Teaching
with Lunsford
Handbooks

Teaching with Lunsford Handbooks

Andrea A. Lunsford

Stanford University

Alyssa O'Brien

Stanford University

Lisa Dresdner

Norwalk Community College

Bedford / St. Martin's

Boston ◆ New York

Manufactured in the United States of America.

6 5 4 3 2 1
f e d c b a

For information, write: Bedford/St. Martin's, 75 Arlington Street, Boston, MA 02116   (617-399-4000)

ISBN: 978-1-4576-0745-5

Acknowledgments

Judy Brady. Excerpt from "Why I Want a Wife." Copyright © 1970 by Judy Brady. Reprinted with the permission of the author.
J. M. S. Careless. Reprinted by permission from *Canada: A Story of Challenge* by J.M.S. Careless (St. Martin's Press, 1964).
"War of 1812." From *The World Book Encyclopedia.* © 1998 World Book, Inc. By permission of the publisher. All rights reserved. www.worldbookonline.com.

Introduction to *Teaching with Lunsford Handbooks*

Congratulations! You are holding the first edition of *Teaching with Lunsford Handbooks*, a manual that will help both first-time teachers and classroom veterans get the most out of any Lunsford handbook. This book offers a treasure trove of resources, developed and classroom-tested with the help of numerous master-teachers, and is applicable to any of the handbooks in the Lunsford family.

In approaching the question of audience for this manual, our first thought was of everyday classroom needs—teaching suggestions, collaborative activities for student writers, and so on. As we began our work, however, we came upon materials and ideas that expanded our original horizons, providing not only the *what* to teach but, more important, the *how* and the *why*.

Our experience mirrors the history of composition scholarship. In the past thirty years, the *what* has changed from a product-oriented approach to a process approach, and now this in turn has become what some refer to as a "post-process" approach. Our teaching today focuses on the material conditions for student writing (and our teaching of it); on the social nature of writing and reading; on an enriched sense of rhetorical situations and the key writing occasions they entail; on changes in the nature, status, and scope of writing; on recently emerging genres of writing; and on the impact of technologies and social media on writing.

Accompanying this shift in what we focus on have been increasingly sophisticated pedagogy and research—the *how*—and greater justification—the *why*. In our experience, the *what* cannot be separated from the *how* and the *why*. This book, therefore, contains materials that respond not only to everyday classroom needs but also to broad pedagogical concerns: how to structure a course and design assignments; sample syllabi for each Lunsford handbook; teaching advice that spans all of a writing class's major topics; activities that reinforce essential reading, writing, and research skills; and more.

Features

Part I: Your Course

The first part of *Teaching with Lunsford Handbooks* features comprehensive advice for developing your course:

- designing a course
- constructing a syllabus
- giving students feedback
- creating effective assignments
- responding to student writing
- using a handbook in the classroom

In addition, this part provides three sample syllabi—one for each handbook—and two sample assignments, along with an assignment template for developing your own.

Part II: Your Teaching

The second part of *Teaching with Lunsford Handbooks* provides classroom-ready materials covering these essential topics: the Top Twenty, rhetorical situations, thesis statements, paragraphs, argument, research, peer review and revision, multimodality, writing in the disciplines, writing for the public, and help for multilingual writers. These resources, classroom-tested and developed over the years by composition specialists, fall into two major categories:

- **Teaching Advice** offers wide-ranging suggestions for how to approach key topics, from useful background information to ways to engage students' attention.
- **Activities** offer concrete suggestions for classroom and small-group work that will help students master important skills.

At the end of every section, *Teaching with Lunsford Handbooks* provides a cross-reference chart that points you to all of the relevant chapters in each of the Lunsford handbooks.

For electronic versions of this book's resources, please visit LunsfordHandbooks.com. For even more resources, please visit the instructor side of the companion Web site for the handbook you are using:

The St. Martin's Handbook: bedfordstmartins.com/smhandbook

The Everyday Writer: bedfordstmartins.com/everydaywriter

EasyWriter: bedfordstmartins.com/easywriter

We would like to thank all the instructors to whom this book is addressed. Everything in this manual was written for you—but in fact much of it, perhaps most, has been inspired by you. We hope that you will find fresh insights and practical suggestions on every page, and that *Teaching with Lunsford Handbooks* will free your time and empower you to create the best writing class possible.

Andrea A. Lunsford
Alyssa O'Brien
Lisa Dresdner

Contents

Introduction to *Teaching with Lunsford Handbooks*   v

| Part I | Your Course | 1 |

Planning the Course   1

Your Writing Course and Your Approach   1

    Student Preparedness and Experience   2

    Student Schedules and Priorities   2

    Student Goals and Majors   2

Organizing the Course Design   3

    Start Your Planning by Identifying the Course Outcomes   3

    Then Determine the Type and Number of Major Assignments   4

    Scaffolding Assignments   4

    Sequencing Assignments   4

Feedback and Assessment   5

    Low-Stakes Writing   5

    Rubrics and Grids   6

    Reflection   7

Figuring Out a Realistic Time Frame   7

The First Day and Beyond   8

Constructing a Syllabus   9

Designing Effective Assignments   11

Aligning Course Learning Outcomes with Assignment Objectives   12

How to Create Effective Writing Prompts   12

    Examples of Some Problematic Prompts   13

Making Assignments Plagiarism-Resistant   14

Creating Steps or Sequencing Your Assignments and Providing Scaffolding   14

Sample Assignments   17

Assignment 1: Letter   17

Assignment 2: Argumentative Essay   20

Assignment Template   23

Sample Syllabi   25

Syllabus 1: *The St. Martin's Handbook*   25

Syllabus 2: *The Everyday Writer*   28

Syllabus 3: *EasyWriter*   36

Responding to Student Writing   39

Know Your Purposes in Responding   39

Types of Comments   40

Know Your Role as a Responder   41

Understand the Student's Perspective   42

The Realities of the Paper Load   43

Utilize Other Types of Feedback   44

Rubrics   44

Individual Conferences   44

Peer Review   45

Student Reflection   45

Using a Handbook   47

Orienting Students to a Handbook   48

Teaching Students to Use a Handbook as a Writing Guide   50

Encouraging Students to Use the Handbook beyond First-Year Composition   55

Part II   Your Teaching   57

The Top Twenty: A Quick Guide to Troubleshooting Your Writing   57

Overview   57

Teaching Advice: Taking a Writing Inventory   58

Teaching Advice: Looking for Strengths in Student Writing   59

Teaching Advice: Learning from Your Errors   59

Teaching Advice: The Top Twenty   60

Activity: The Top Twenty   61

Rhetorical Situations   63

Overview   63

Teaching Advice: Understanding Rhetorical Situations   63

Teaching Advice: Understanding Academic Assignments   63

Choices about Topics   64

Rhetorical Stance   64

Activity: Thinking about Topics 64

Activity: Purposes for Academic Writing 64

Teaching Advice: Prewriting 65

Teaching Advice: Considering Audiences 65

Activity: Audiences for Formal and Academic Writing 66

Activity: Specific Audiences and Peer Response 66

Teaching Advice: Analyze Your Position as a Writer or Speaker ... 66

Activity: Analyze Your Position as a Writer or Speaker 67

Activity: Tone and Style 1 67

Activity: Tone and Style 2 67

Resources 68

Thesis 69

  Overview 69

    Teaching Advice: Exploring a Topic 69

      Brainstorming 70

      Freewriting and Looping 70

      Clustering 70

    Activity: Drafting a Working Thesis 70

    Teaching Advice: Gathering Information 71

    Activity: Gathering Information 71

    Activity: Organizing Verbal and Visual Information 1 71

    Activity: Organizing Verbal and Visual Information 2 72

    Teaching Advice: Planning 72

    Teaching Advice: Drafting 72

    Resources 73

Paragraphs 75

  Overview 75

    Teaching Advice: Creating Strong Paragraphs 75

    Activity: Creating Strong Paragraphs 75

    Teaching Advice: Writing Unified Paragraphs 76

    Activity: Writing Unified Paragraphs 1 76

    Activity: Writing Unified Paragraphs 2 76

    Teaching Advice: Developing Paragraphs 77

      Determining Paragraph Length 77

    Activity: Developing Paragraphs 1 77

    Activity: Developing Paragraphs 2 78

    Teaching Advice: Making Paragraphs Coherent 78

      Repetition for Coherent Paragraphs 78

      Repetition and Parallel Structure 79

      Transitional Devices 79

    Activity: Making Paragraphs Coherent 1—Transitional Devices ... 79

    Activity: Making Paragraphs Coherent 2—Organization ... 80

Teaching Advice: Linking Paragraphs Together   80

Teaching Advice: Writing Special-Purpose Paragraphs   80

Activity: Writing Special-Purpose Paragraphs—Conclusions   81

Resources   81

Argument   83

Critical Reading: Overview   83

Teaching Advice: Critical Reading   83

Activity: Previewing a Text   84

Activity: Reading and Annotating a Text   84

Activity: Analyzing a Text   85

Analyzing Arguments: Overview   85

Activity: Thinking Critically about Argument   85

Activity: Considering Cultural Contexts   86

Activity: Reading Emotional, Ethical, and Logical Appeals 1   86

Activity: Reading Emotional, Ethical, and Logical Appeals 2   86

Activity: Identifying Elements of an Argument   87

Teaching Advice: Identifying Fallacies   87

Activity: Identifying Fallacies 1   87

Activity: Identifying Fallacies 2   87

Activity: Analyzing Arguments   87

Constructing Arguments: Overview   88

Activity: Formulating a Working Thesis   88

Activity: Shape Your Appeal to Your Audience   89

Teaching Advice: Making Ethical Appeals   89

Fairness toward Counterarguments   89

Activity: Making Ethical Appeals—Common Ground   89

Teaching Advice: Making Logical Appeals   90

Examples, Precedents, and Narratives   90

Authority and Testimony   90

Causes and Effects   90

Inductive and Deductive Reasoning   91

Teaching Advice: Making Emotional Appeals   91

Activity: Making Emotional Appeals—Visuals   91

Activity: Using Sources in an Argument   92

Activity: Organizing an Argument   92

Resources   93

Research   95

Preparing for a Research Project: Overview   95

Teaching Advice: Considering the Research Process   95

Activity: Considering the Research Process   96

Teaching Advice: Analyzing the Assignment   96

Teaching Advice: Narrowing a Topic 96

Activity: Narrowing a Topic 97

Activity: Moving from Research Question to Hypothesis 97

Teaching Advice: Making a Preliminary Research Plan 97

Teaching Advice: Keeping a Research Log 98

Teaching Advice: Moving from Hypothesis to Working Thesis 98

Conducting Research: Overview 99

Teaching Advice: Differentiating Kinds of Sources 99

Activity: Differentiating Kinds of Sources 100

Teaching Advice: Using the Library to Get Started 100

Teaching Advice: Finding Library Resources 101

Activity: Finding Library Resources 101

Teaching Advice: Conducting Internet Research 101

Teaching Advice: Conducting Field Research 102

Observation 102

Activity: Conducting Field Research 1—Interviews 102

Activity: Conducting Field Research 2—Surveys 103

Evaluating Sources and Taking Notes: Overview 103

Teaching Advice: Using Sources to Meet a Need 103

Activity: Using Sources to Meet a Need 104

Teaching Advice: Keeping a Working Bibliography 104

Teaching Advice: Evaluating Usefulness and Credibility 104

Activity: Reading and Interpreting Sources 105

Activity: Synthesizing Sources 1 108

Activity: Synthesizing Sources 2 108

Teaching Advice: Taking Notes and Annotating Sources 109

Electronic Note-Taking 109

Quotations 109

Paraphrases 109

Activity: Taking Notes and Annotating Sources 1—Paraphrase 110

Activity: Taking Notes and Annotating Sources 2—Summary 110

Integrating Sources into Your Writing: Overview 111

Activity: Deciding Whether to Quote, Paraphrase, or Summarize 111

Teaching Advice: Working with Quotations 111

Teaching Advice: Summarizing 112

Activity: Working with Quotations, Paraphrases, and Summaries 112

Teaching Advice: Checking for Excessive Use of Source Material 112

Activity: Integrating Sources 113

Acknowledging Sources and Avoiding Plagiarism: Overview 113

Teaching Advice: Understanding Reasons to Acknowledge Sources 114

Activity: Knowing Which Sources to Acknowledge 114

Teaching Advice: Maintaining Academic Integrity and Avoiding Plagiarism 114

Activity: Considering Your Intellectual Property 116

Writing a Research Project: Overview 116

Teaching Advice: Refining Your Plans 116

Activity: Working on a Thesis Statement 117

Teaching Advice: Organizing Information 117

Outlining 118

Activity: Organizing Information 118

Activity: Outlining 118

Teaching Advice: Drafting 118

Activity: Introductions and Conclusions 119

Resources 120

Peer Review and Revision 123

Reviewing and Revising: Overview 123

Teaching Advice: Rereading Your Draft 123

Activity: Rereading Your Draft 124

Teaching Advice: Reviewing Peer Writers 124

Activity: Reviewing Peer Writers 1 125

Activity: Reviewing Peer Writers 2 125

Teaching Advice: Learning from Instructor Comments 126

Purpose 126

Paragraph Structure 126

Documentation 127

For MLA Citation 127

Activity: Revising with Peer and Instructor Comments 1 127

Activity: Revising with Peer and Instructor Comments 2 128

Activity: Revising with Peer and Instructor Comments 3 128

Teaching Advice: Revising Thesis and Support 128

Activity: Rethinking Organization 1 129

Activity: Rethinking Organization 2 129

Activity: Revising Titles 1 129

Activity: Revising Titles 2 129

Activity: Revising Introductions 130

Activity: Revising Conclusions 130

Teaching Advice: Revising Paragraphs, Sentences, Words, and Tone 131

Revising Words 131

Revising Tone 131

Activity: Revising Paragraphs 1 132

Activity: Revising Paragraphs 2 132

Activity: Revising Paragraphs 3 132

Activity: Revising Sentences   132

Editing and Reflecting: Overview   133

Activity: Editing   133

Activity: Sentence Openings   133

Teaching Advice: Sentence Length   133

Activity: Opening with It *and* There   133

Teaching Advice: Proofreading the Final Draft   134

Teaching Advice: A Student's Revised Draft   134

Teaching Advice: Portfolios   134

Activity: Portfolios   135

Teaching Advice: Reflective Statements   136

Resources   137

Multimodality   139

Thinking about Visuals and Media: Overview   139

Teaching Advice: Visuals, Media, and Design   139

Teaching Advice: Thinking Critically about Visuals   139

Teaching Advice: Working with Visuals   140

Teaching Advice: Analyzing Visual Arguments   140

Activity: Analyzing Visual Arguments   140

Teaching Advice: Thinking about Genre   141

Design for Writing: Overview   141

Teaching Advice: Questions about Design   142

Teaching Advice: Document Design   142

Teaching Advice: Planning a Visual Structure   142

Activity: Formatting   143

Teaching Advice: Planning Visuals   143

Activity: Planning Visuals   144

Online Texts: Overview   144

Teaching Advice: Planning an Online Text   145

Activity: Planning an Online Text   145

Teaching Advice: Considering Types of Online Texts   145

Activity: Considering Types of Online Texts   146

Teaching Advice: Examining Features of Online Texts   146

Activity: Examining Features of Online Texts   146

Activity: Thinking Critically about Argument in Online Texts   146

Teaching Advice: Putting Your Text Together   147

Teaching Advice: Formal and Informal Electronic Communications   147

Teaching Advice: Composing Academic and Professional Messages   148

Teaching Advice: Writing for Less Formal Situations   149

Activity: Writing for Less Formal Situations — 149

Oral and Multimedia Presentations: Overview — 149

Teaching Advice: Considering Assignment, Purpose, and Audience for Presentations — 150

Activity: Composing for Oral Presentations 1 — 150

Activity: Composing for Oral Presentations 2 — 151

Teaching Advice: Practicing Presentations — 151

Activity: Practicing Presentations — 151

Activity: Evaluating Presentations — 152

Resources — 152

Writing in the Disciplines — 155

Writing in Any Discipline: Overview — 155

Activity: Academic Work in Any Discipline — 155

Activity: Understanding Academic Assignments — 155

Activity: Learning Specialized Vocabulary — 156

Activity: Following Disciplinary Style — 156

Activity: Using Appropriate Evidence — 156

Writing for the Humanities: Overview — 157

Teaching Advice: Writing Texts in the Humanities — 157

Activity: Writing Texts in the Humanities 1 — 157

Activity: Writing Texts in the Humanities 2 — 157

Writing for the Social Sciences: Overview — 157

Teaching Advice: Reading Texts in the Social Sciences — 158

Teaching Advice: Writing Texts in the Social Sciences — 158

Activity: Writing Texts in the Social Sciences 1 — 158

Activity: Writing Texts in the Social Sciences 2 — 159

Writing for the Natural and Applied Sciences: Overview — 159

Teaching Advice: Reading Texts in the Natural and Applied Sciences — 159

Activity: Reading Texts in the Natural and Applied Sciences — 159

Activity: Writing Texts in the Natural and Applied Sciences — 160

Writing for Business: Overview — 160

Teaching Advice: Reading Texts for Business — 160

Activity: Reading Texts for Business — 161

Activity: Writing Texts for Business — 161

Activity: Writing Memos — 161

Activity: Writing Résumés — 161

Resources — 162

Writing for the Public — 163

Overview — 163

Activity: Identifying Your Audience — 163

Activity: Connecting with Your Audience   163

Resources   164

Helping Multilingual Writers   165

Writing in U.S. Academic Contexts: Overview   165

Teaching Advice: Meeting Expectations for U.S. Academic Writing   165

Activity: Understanding Genre Conventions   166

Teaching Advice: Adapting Structures and Phrases from a Genre   166

Teaching Advice: Strategies for Learning from Search Engines   166

Activity: Strategies for Learning from Search Engines   167

Clauses and Sentences   167

Activity: Clauses and Sentences 1   167

Activity: Clauses and Sentences 2   168

Nouns and Noun Phrases: Overview   168

Activity: Using Count and Noncount Nouns   169

Activity: Using Articles   169

Activity: Using Nouns in Specific Languages   169

Verbs and Verb Phrases: Overview   169

Activity: Verbs and Verb Phrases   170

Prepositions and Prepositional Phrases: Overview   170

Activity: Using Prepositions Idiomatically   170

Resources   171

Planning the Course

Your Writing Course and Your Approach

Whether a college or university requires one composition course or a two-course sequence, a common misconception is that the writing course should teach students how to write for all of their subsequent college classes. While there is some truth to that view, in as much as composition instructors should be teaching writing skills and strategies that are transferable across many disciplines, addressing *all* the skills necessary to be a successful writer in all future academic courses would be impossible in just one or two twelve- to fourteen-week semesters. Moreover, doing so would be detrimental to the student; you would not be able to spend sufficient time on any one topic.

The first step, then, is to find out from the department chair how many weeks your course semester lasts and whether the department has a specific philosophy that will shape your approach to the course. Most English departments now embrace writing as a process and, therefore, ask that you incorporate revision as one of the writing strategies and build multiple drafts into the assignment and grading process. Because most college writing is now done as a response to or in dialogue with a text, instructors engage students as both writers and readers and help them make connections in their thinking between writing and reading. Therefore, by grouping readings together thematically or by having an overarching or essential question to frame the course (e.g., "How do stories shape the world around us?" or "How do gender roles limit individual choices?") you might be able to make easier decisions about what readings to assign when planning your course. Even before you choose the readings, though, you need to ask yourself *why* you are assigning the readings and what you hope to accomplish with them: are you assigning them to be used as models of good writing or are you assigning them to generate ideas and provoke questions? Additionally, many English departments use a portfolio process for assessment, and this may affect the grading scale you use.

The second step is to find out as much as you can about the environment in which you will be teaching; this includes both the classroom and the students. Will you be teaching in a traditional classroom with regular desks? A seminar room with tables? A computer lab where every student will have a computer? Or a "smart" classroom where you'll have a computer station with Internet access but students will have only desks? Or a combination of any of these on alternating days? The type of classroom often shapes the kinds of activities that are most productive on any given day.

Rarely does a "typical" college classroom that you might have enjoyed as an undergraduate exist anymore, and discovering as much as you can about the kinds of students you will be teaching will also help you to be prepared with effective instructional strategies and assignments when you begin the semester. Your department chair, other instructors, and the college's home Web site are good resources for finding out about your particular student demographics. Questions you may want to ask include the following:

Student Preparedness and Experience

- Are the majority of students coming straight from high school or are they older, nontraditional students? This might determine their familiarity with academic writing as well as with technology.

- Does your college have open enrollment or is it selective? How are students placed into your class? Do they take a placement exam? Do some pass into your course from developmental courses or ESL courses? If so, will they need extra help for specific language issues?

- What is the social and cultural diversity of your classroom? What kinds of background knowledge and experiences from your students can you draw on to inform your lessons?

- What resources are available at your college for your students? Is there a writing center or lab? tutors? online assistance or resources? What kinds of services do the librarians offer? Librarians love to help in a variety of ways and are often open to suggestions that go far beyond traditional library orientation, such as running workshops to help with term paper research, informational literacy, or a range of other topics you may want to explore with your students. You will want to familiarize yourself with these resources so that you can refer your students to them and, when necessary, build them into your assignments.

Student Schedules and Priorities

- Are most of the students full-time or part-time?
- Do many of the students work? If so, about how many hours per week?
- Will you have any student athletes who will be missing a significant number of classes?

Student Goals and Majors

- Are your students all in similar majors or programs? If so, you might structure your readings and assignments accordingly. Are they honor students?
- Are all your students all in school for the same purpose? (Consider, for instance, degree-track, transfer status, and career goals.)
- Will your students be taking any writing-intensive courses after yours?

Organizing the Course Design

One of the joys of teaching college is that your classroom is your domain. Of course, if you are new to this territory, that joy comes with a certain amount of terror, especially with a writing class where the subject being taught is learned recursively and your students will have a wide range of skills and abilities: What do you teach first? How much reading should you assign? How many papers should you assign? What kinds of papers should they be? How many revisions should you build in? Will feedback come solely from you or will you incorporate peer review? Should you include journal writing? How do you know when students are learning? Are quizzes appropriate for a composition class? What kinds of assessment measures will you use?

Frequently, course design is driven by *content* (in this case, writing) and, to add coherence, a *theme* (gender roles, justice in society, education). *Types* of assignments are often chosen based on the readings and on what is required by the department or what an instructor is most comfortable working with (often based on his or her own experience as a learner). Thus, assignments might range from a series of rhetorical modes (narrative, persuasive, analytical, descriptive, etc.); genre-based writing (types of writing that are usually associated with a social purpose, that are audience and purpose driven, and that incorporate specific conventions such as letters, editorials, brochures, etc.); a progression from personal narrative to argumentation; or some combination of these. And while all these kinds of assignments have value, they are often given randomly with little regard to the ways in which they might be working together to produce effective learning. What is more beneficial to the student is to move forward through the semester through *backward design*.

Backward design, popularized by Grant Wiggins and Jay McTighe in their 1998 book *Understanding by Design*, focuses on three main points that you are most likely to consider when constructing a class, but it asks you to think of your end goals *first* and then determine the most effective way to reach them.

1. End results: What do you want the students to have learned by the end of your course?
2. Assessment: How will you determine whether the students have learned these skills? What will be the evidence?
3. Methods: What instructional activities and assignments will best lead to these results?

Start Your Planning by Identifying the Course Outcomes

More and more accreditation standards include requiring colleges to list course outcomes in their course syllabi, so find out if your department has standard outcomes that your students should be able to demonstrate. In contrast to course *objectives*, which are usually listed as topics to be covered during a semester, course *outcomes* are framed as what students should be able to demonstrate and how they will do so, which defines for you the learning goals as well as a way to measure whether the skill or concept has been learned. You might also find out the next class that students are likely to take after yours. Knowing how your course aligns with other courses might also help you decide on the types of writing you will assign for the optimum learning environment.

Then Determine the Type and Number of Major Assignments

Typically in a twelve- to fourteen-week semester course, instructors assign anywhere between four to six papers, depending on the length of the papers, the types of assignments, and whether the course requires a research paper, which requires more time than other types of assignments. Given that each paper will undergo the entire writing process, including prewriting, drafting, revising, and editing, and given the time involved with some of the instructional activities, you may want to opt for fewer major assignments and more minor or low-stakes writing assignments that build up to the more formal assignments.

As backward design suggests, the types of assignments will be driven by what you want your students to have learned by the end of the course. If, for instance, one of the course outcomes is for students to incorporate multiple sources in an argumentative paper that is five to seven pages long, you might position that assignment at the end of the semester and choose to start with an assignment that asks them to integrate only one source. But even that initial assignment will require students to have learned the basics of writing effective theses, paragraph development, and correct quote integration and citation. While the writing process itself is often messy at best, the teaching of the writing process certainly doesn't have to be! What is crucial is careful planning and thinking through the whole course design; scaffolding assignments so as to increase students' confidence and help them become independent learners and writers; and sequencing assignments so as to build on one another and students' prior and learned knowledge.

Scaffolding Assignments

Just as scaffolding in the construction world provides temporary external support to enable workers to get to parts of a building they would not otherwise be able to access, scaffolding in instructional design provides support for students to increase their familiarity and confidence with a concept or skill until they can implement or apply it independently. Scaffolding methods include modeling, collaboration, individual conferencing, and providing direct access to external resources—whether they are the handbook itself, the library, or online tutorials and guides. The keys to successful scaffolding are that it be done with intentionality, that it be adaptive to the students' needs, and that it gradually be limited so that students learn to provide their own means of internal support in their growth as independent learners and writers.

Sequencing Assignments

Creating assignments that are sequenced, or connected, in a variety of ways provides a number of benefits for the students:

- Students understand the bigger picture of what they are learning in the course, helping them to see connections in their learning process.

- Students are able to see their progress more visibly and to understand how their work builds on itself, rather than viewing each assignment as a separate and isolated exercise.
- Students are encouraged to do critical thinking through a sustained focus on revision and consideration of multiple perspectives.

More complex ways of sequencing assignments that might shape your syllabus include the following:

- Connect a series of assignments by degree of complexity or mode of discourse, such as moving from a journal response to a reading, to a summary of that reading, to a position or argumentative paper based on the reading.
- Connect a series of assignments by changing the audience: move from personal to public, from an audience of peers to one of experts.
- Connect a series of assignments by topic so that students engage more fully with different perspectives and then must evaluate the views, synthesize them, and adopt their own position.
- Connect a series of assignments over time, starting with a personal statement of understanding of an issue and returning to that position later after reading more on the topic. This can lead to an analysis of the initial stance based on the new knowledge and experience.

Examples of other assignment sequences and scaffolding are given in the next chapter, Designing Effective Assignments.

Feedback and Assessment

As you think through your course design, you must also consider what benchmarks you will set to assess students' learning progress. Doing so is important both for the students and for yourself, as you want to know when and how to adjust your teaching to increase your students' learning. Identifying these assessment markers before the start of the semester is crucial in planning the course. Of course, not everything is worth assessing, and sometimes you will simply want to integrate some low-stakes writing activities as a way to help students get involved in their topics and become more fluid and fluent in their writing.

Low-Stakes Writing

Low-stakes writing is frequent, informal writing—often done in class in brief amounts of time—and is designed not to produce excellent pieces of strong writing but, rather, to engage students in writing at little to no risk (since no grade is attached to it). This type of writing accomplishes several things:

- As students become more fluent in their writing, they also become more comfortable with it, so that they approach formal assignments with more confidence.

- Students begin to grapple with their subject, to wade through sometimes muddled thinking; and they learn that writing can become a way of thinking through their ideas.
- Students move from relying on what the instructor is looking for to asking themselves "What am *I* looking for?" One of the results is that they become more internally motivated.
- It allows them to experience writing with their minds focused solely on the topic and the issues rather than how the writing will be evaluated.

Depending on how you use a low-stakes writing activity, it can provide a way to assess how students are responding to and understanding the material.

Rubrics and Grids

Rubrics and grids are helpful and efficient tools to assess your students' writing, and these methods communicate your expectations clearly to students so that they know precisely what they should focus on in a given assignment. Providing a rubric or a grid at the same time an assignment is given provides a guide and additional scaffolding for students, enhancing their abilities to learn the necessary skills for that specific assignment. A rubric is usually more detailed than a grid, but both provide an opportunity for quick and helpful feedback and can be adjusted to what you want to emphasize in an assignment. While both offer some kind of ranking, neither needs *necessarily* to be tied to a conventional grade.

Example of a rubric designed to teach students peer review in an online format

Criteria	Exemplary	Really Good	Average	Poor
Responsiveness to Peers	Replies demonstrate thoughtful engagement; clear connections are made to skills we have learned; suggestions for improvement and strengthening are concrete and specific.	Replies show engagement; some connections to skills we have learned are made; suggestions for improvement and strengthening are somewhat specific.	Replies are vague and/or brief; few connections to skills we have learned are made; suggestions for improvement and strengthening are abstract and vague.	Replies lack thoughtful engagement; no connections to skills we have learned are made; no suggestions for improvement and strengthening are given.
Comments:				

Example of a grid for a first draft of a paper (criteria would be tied to purposes of the assignment)

Strong	OK	Weak	CRITERIA
			Clear, arguable thesis
			Introduction that "hooks" the reader
			Organization, structure, guiding the reader
			Content, insights, thinking, grappling with topic
Comments:			

Reflection

Reflection is another way to assess students' understanding, and, importantly, reflection is recognized more and more as central to deepening the learning process. However, most students have not had a great deal of experience with structured reflective practice. To help students build toward a substantive reflective statement that might be used to accompany a portfolio, have them practice shorter reflections on their growth as learners and writers throughout the semester. These assignments can be done through journals, as self-evaluations prior to handing in a draft of an assignment, and/or as observations of the feedback they have received. Creating a habit of reflection will allow both you and the student to see what and where learning and understanding is occurring and what kinds of adjustments might be needed in the course of the semester. The record of growth will also serve as a guide at the end of the semester for a more comprehensive assessment of learning.

Figuring Out a Realistic Time Frame

Without careful planning, a semester can get away from you too quickly; before you know it, you are buried in a mass of new and revised papers, and the end of the semester is just around the corner. If only figuring out the actual schedule were as simple as dividing the number of weeks by the number of papers! But the reality is that different kinds of assignments demand different time frames, and furthermore, inevitably something unforeseen will come up during the semester that will throw your schedule off a bit—whether it is that students need more time to grasp a complex skill, or that a weather-related event causes a class to be canceled. Creating some time and space for flexibility in your semester schedule can easily be done by allowing the last week or two to be devoted to workshops focusing on putting the final touches on papers or portfolios or, depending on how your class is structured, to lessons in style. That way, if you need to encroach on those days for other, more basic skills, you have room to do so.

Since building revision into the writing process is central to this guide, you need to determine how much time is realistic for students to engage in the entire writing process, including the review process to provide the necessary feedback for a substantive revision. You will want to strike a balance between work that is done in class and work done outside of class; and you will also want to look at how your reading and writing assignments are structured. Consider whether writing a draft over a weekend makes more sense than writing it during the week; and, especially at the beginning of the semester, build in plenty of opportunities for feedback to reward motivation. Try to be realistic about students' lives as well as your own!

The First Day and Beyond

You should strive to accomplish three primary goals on the first day of class:

1. Introductions; by way of introducing yourself and the students—often through an informal icebreaker—you set the tone for the entire semester.

2. Overview of the syllabus: students will be receiving anywhere from one to five different syllabi for the semester, depending on how many courses they are taking, and you want to be sure they know the salient points of *your* syllabus; so take some time to go over it with them. You might have them talk about certain parts of the syllabus in small groups and ask any questions that arise. Some instructors have students write a statement on the *second* day of class confirming they have read the syllabus and understand the policies and procedures of the class. Others give a short quiz on the syllabus (but this means you would also have to grade the quiz, and you need to determine whether you want to count that quiz in the grade distribution). The point is that students need to understand that they are responsible for knowing what is in the syllabus and that the syllabus is their "contract" in the class. **Note**: When you review your syllabus with your students, clarify for them how you have set up the daily schedule for reading and writing assignments. For instance, when you list a reading assignment on a given day, do you mean for students to read that as homework for the following day or to have read it and to be prepared to discuss it for that day? Instructors often mean different things, and you want to be clear with your schedule from the outset.

3. Set aside at least thirty minutes for students to write a short, diagnostic essay in class (assuring them that it is ungraded), which will give you an opportunity to see what kinds of issues you will need to address over the course of the semester. What is most important with this sample of writing is that you return it to the students within a week with your feedback. Include a positive comment about the quality, voice, structure,

or content of the writing as well as any feedback about one or two areas you think the student will need to start strengthening right away. This immediate feedback helps to establish a relationship of trust and respect from the start that will encourage continual dialogue throughout the semester to lead to student success.

Constructing a Syllabus

A syllabus is usually divided into two main parts: the first part, which lists the required information about the course and policies and procedures, is your class contract, so when constructing your syllabus the old adage "less is more" does not apply. In fact, you probably cannot have too much information in this portion of your syllabus. Students will refer to this document throughout the semester to reference their upcoming assignments, and you may want to refer to it when faced with a behavioral issue or a student handing in a late paper. The second part of the syllabus is your class schedule, which includes the actual dates of your class meetings, readings, homework, and paper assignments. This latter part will often undergo some modification as the semester progresses to account for unforeseen student needs, school or class cancellations (snow days? fire drills?), or campus events that you may want to take advantage of. Therefore, you may want to add a note about the possibility of the syllabus being modified as well as insert a footer with an "effective as of" date on it.

Many colleges now have standard course syllabi to meet accreditation requirements, so you may be given a template by your department chair that names specific components that must be included. Even if you have a template to use, you might want to compare it against the following list:

The following items should always be included on a syllabus:

- course information, number, section, meeting days, times, and place
- your contact information, including any office hours
- course description (usually from the course catalog) and course outcomes
- course prerequisites
- required texts and materials (folders? flash drive?)
- grading scale and distribution of assignments
- attendance policy*
- a statement on academic integrity*
- a statement regarding students with disabilities who may need accommodations*
- late paper or makeup work policy
- a statement about syllabus modification
- footer with an effective date (to allow for any revisions you might make to your class schedule of assignments)

* The college may have policies and procedures associated with these items, which would most likely be found in the student handbook.

- class schedule (including readings, assignments, and major dates that affect a student's academic life such as add/drop and withdrawal dates)

Additional information to include on your syllabus would be policies and procedures that establish the guidelines for behavior and expectations in your classroom:

- a list of resources and their hours (writing and/or tutoring center, multilanguage services, online tutoring services, the library, etc.)
- a statement on cell phones and other electronic devices
- formatting directions for papers and/or academic conventions
- a grading rubric

The sample syllabi shown on pages 25–38 are for fourteen-week, process-based composition courses for traditional students and use a portfolio for an exit assessment. Note how the assignments are sequenced to build on one another and how the handbook is integrated throughout to support the lessons. (Also note that the first and third syllabi are more skeletal and don't include all of the information described in this section.)

Consider posting your syllabus and other relevant handouts on a Web-based shell for easy access when students lose their copies, which will inevitably happen!

Designing Effective Assignments

Assignments can take a wide range of forms about a multitude of topics, but one thing has become clear in recent years: a direct relationship exists between an *effective assignment* and the opportunity to produce *good writing*.

Think of all the things an assignment might do. It can create opportunities for students to:

- demonstrate writing skills they have learned;
- illustrate a new understanding of an issue or topic;
- reflect on their learning and/or growth as writers;
- explore connections with other concepts or courses;
- generate more ideas or new ways of thinking through ideas for a complex assignment;
- argue or persuade or inform or entertain an authentic audience.

And assignments can encourage creativity and the development of a strong writer's voice.

However, one assignment cannot do *all* of these things, so the first step in designing an *effective* assignment is to determine what objectives you want to accomplish, which should always align with a course outcome. At the beginning of a semester, with novice writers, you may want to start with the most fundamental objectives, such as comprehending a college-level article or essay and formulating a thesis that is supported through well-developed paragraphs. As the semester progresses and your students become more advanced writers, your assignment objectives will adjust accordingly, so that near the end of the semester, objectives might include the evaluation of and integration of more than one source in an argumentative essay.

Aligning Course Learning Outcomes with Assignment Objectives

The following chart shows a sample of learning activities that progress from more basic to more advanced:

Course Learning Outcome	Assignments and Objectives
Construct an effective thesis that is developed and supported with specific examples and details.	Formulate a thesis in response to an analytical prompt and write the essay by developing unified and coherent paragraphs.
Engage in a dialogue with a text; integrate the student's own ideas with those of others.	Summarize an article, clarifying the author's argument. Then write a response to the author. Posing actual questions and answers can help them see how they can be in "dialogue" with a writer. Emphasize that the student and author are each positioned somewhere along a continuum.
Develop the ability to critique your own and others' work.	Conduct a peer-review workshop with specific and focused questions to answer. This might be followed by a summary of the feedback given and an explanation of how that feedback will be used to revise the paper.
Understand that writing is a process.	Draft, revise, and edit a paper.
Quote and paraphrase source material according to MLA.	Use parenthetical citations and signal phrases to integrate quotes and to paraphrase effectively; include a list of works cited.
Locate, evaluate, and synthesize secondary source material.	Articulate a clear position that can be supported by research; find at least four different sources and write an annotation of each. Choose three to integrate into your paper and explain why they are effective and credible sources.

How to Create Effective Writing Prompts

Effective prompts communicate your expectations to your students. They should *always* be written out and explained in class to ensure that all the terms are understood. Additionally, having an assignment on paper allows students to refer to it throughout the writing process and helps those who may be assisting the student (for example, tutors in the writing center) to be more effective.

While writing assignments will naturally be tailored to the needs of your students and your curriculum, you should be as specific as possible when creating them:

- Identify clear objectives that link to one or more learning outcomes.

- Create a meaningful task that corresponds to the goals; often referred to as "authentic" writing prompts, assignments with real-world application or scenarios help to make the writing more meaningful to the students. Different genres provide useful opportunities for students to understand different rhetorical contexts and help them understand their roles as writers and how to define their audiences.

- Outline specific steps that point to the desired outcome; adjust the length of your prompt appropriately for the length and value of the assignment.

- Set challenging but realistic expectations in terms of form, content, and deadlines.

- Provide clear evaluation criteria.

- Use models or samples—either attached to the assignment or in your pedagogical strategy.

- Encourage self-reflection with each assignment.

- Provide a list of resources or tips, such as specific pages in the handbook, to assist students in the writing process.

The type of phrasing you use in crafting your assignments will be determined by several factors, including how you might be sequencing assignments throughout the semester, whether the department requires you to use specific kinds of assignments, and your student population (developmental, advanced, adult, etc.). Whatever key terms you use (*analyze, argue, compare, synthesize*), be sure to clarify the meaning in class and, whenever possible, provide a sample paper. Terms such as *explore* or *discuss* don't provide very much direction; nor does the rather general imperative "Write about XX."

Sometimes seeing a problematic assignment prompt helps you understand the ways you can design your assignments more effectively. If an assignment is too extreme—either too abstract or too complicated—then students might have trouble knowing how to approach their writing. The result—vague, meandering, and obtuse writing—will only frustrate both you and the students in the end. So taking care to think through what you want your students to accomplish and the most effective steps to help them do so will serve you well in the long run.

Examples of Some Problematic Prompts

> Write about an issue that means a lot to you and with which you are familiar. Explore this issue and how it has evolved. Do not use outside resources; use only your own knowledge and feelings for your support.

This prompt is far too vague and general; a student wouldn't know where to begin.

> In his essay "The Insufficiency of Honesty," Stephen Carter writes that Americans have gone too far to the extreme and "discover[ed] the absolute minimum obligation that we have to others as a result of our promises" (323). He adds that "here in America, people seem to spend their time thinking of even cleverer ways to avoid their obligations, instead of doing what integrity commands and fulfilling them" (323). Show with examples how this is so.

To what does "this" refer? What kind of essay is a student supposed to write?

Making Assignments Plagiarism-Resistant

While some colleges and universities subscribe to various online tools that are able to find plagiarized passages, what is more beneficial to the student is to create assignments that make plagiarism difficult to do. Here are some strategies to follow:

- Make your assignments specific to the readings and discussions done in your class, especially if you ask students to make connections between or among them.

- Limit research paper topics or resources; require students to relate a local component to their research project and to require an interview. Not only does this help to deter plagiarism, but it also makes the project more relevant to the student.

- Sequence each assignment in such a way that some of the writing is done in class and in smaller parts so that students can develop and build on their own ideas gradually. This also allows you to reward students with early feedback, thus providing more motivation.

- Longer and more complex assignments might involve planning and analysis of the progress and any challenges.

- Ask for annotation of resources and justification for their use.

- Use examples and frequent practice of paraphrase and summary in collaborative ways so students can learn a range of strategies from one another.

- Point out ways that professionals synthesize sources, emphasizing the way the thinking is done as well as the documentation.

Creating Steps or Sequencing Your Assignments and Providing Scaffolding

You can sequence your assignments in a wide range of ways. The most basic form of sequencing an assignment is to create separate steps for brainstorming, drafting, writing, and revising the paper. Even these individual steps, though, can be done in a variety of ways—in class, out of class, informally and formally. The game plans and activities in *The Everyday Writer* are excellent strategies to integrate into any stage of the assignment sequence.

Longer and more complex assignments can build in journals, reflections, or other low-stakes writing that allow students to reflect on their progress, discoveries, and frustrations. This provides an opportunity for you or their peers to offer early help with feedback or alternative strategies and approaches.

Assignment: mid-semester argumentative essay integrating one source—three-week sequence

Instruction	Student Tasks
Introduce assignment and review the sample paper; review freewriting, clustering, questioning, and listing in handbook.	Students engage in two different methods of exploring ideas individually; work in pairs to exchange feedback and deepen ideas.
Review thesis statements in handbook.	Formulate a working thesis; three to five volunteers to write thesis on board and discuss as class strengths/weaknesses; work in pairs to strengthen thesis and start outlining supporting points.
Review argumentative structure in handbook and tips on organization.	In-class writing: develop supporting points more thoroughly and begin to frame them in a logical way; instructor circulates among individuals.
Review paragraph development; introductions and conclusions; discuss revision—refer to your own writing process as an example.	Bring three copies of first draft to class; small-group peer review with a focus on organization and paragraph development. Read intros aloud at end of class to identify ones with the strongest "hook."
Review quote integration/citation in handbook; discuss plagiarism.	Bring draft #2 to class; focus on paragraphs with quotes in them. Work on works-cited page.
Go over proofreading strategies; provide list of three reflective questions to answer.	Bring final revised essay to class; proofread one last time. Write a reflective paragraph to accompany the assignment.

Sample Assignments

Assignment 1: Letter

ENG101: Composition

Writing Assignment: Letter

Purpose of the assignment:

1. To demonstrate awareness of audience, purpose, and tone
2. To demonstrate that you have paid attention to the speaker(s) and considered their comments thoughtfully
3. To demonstrate that you have learned the proper formatting of a letter
4. To show that you know how to proofread carefully

To write this assignment effectively, you will need to do the following:

1. Pay close attention to the presentation.
2. Ask a specific question of the presenter, or listen carefully to those who do.
3. Get the name, title, and an address of the presenter. (I may be able to help out here!)

Prompt:

Your assignment is to write a letter to the presenter. In this letter, do the following:

1. Thank the person for presenting.
2. Summarize what you learned in the presentation, and in that summary address the question and answer from your attendance.
3. Pose a larger, more general, philosophical question in your letter. This kind of question shows that you are thinking beyond the limits of a short presentation—that you are able to relate the presentation to other areas of life. You do not need to answer the larger question you ask; in fact, it may not have a direct answer. But you need to be thoughtful and reflective about the importance and significance of this question.

This shows a different kind of assignment. While it seems rather prescriptive in the prompt itself, it actually lends itself to creative and critical thinking because students are usually so interested in such different things during presentations and they approach the speakers from different backgrounds and experiences. It also is a very practical sort of assignment that will be applicable in many future situations.

Due dates:

Wednesday: Draft for peer review
Monday: Final copy, signed and ready to be mailed!

Resources:

Guidelines for formatting letters are on pages 555–57 in the fourth edition of *The Everyday Writer*. Pay close attention to the spacing and follow this format carefully!

A sample letter follows.

Evaluation:

Criteria	Excellent	Average	Needs Substantial Improvement
Audience/Purpose	Vocabulary, style, and diction are effective and appropriate for purpose and audience	Vocabulary, style, and diction are okay for purpose and audience	Vocabulary, style, and diction are inappropriate for purpose and audience
Sincerity/ Thoughtfulness	Clear summary of presentation; excellent address of a Q&A; thoughtful philosophical question	At least one of the following is either not clear or missing: summary of presentation; address of a Q&A; a thoughtful philosophical question	More than one of the following is not clear or missing: summary of presentation; address of a Q&A; a philosophical question
Proper Formatting	Spacing, justification, and margins are all correct	Some mistakes in spacing, justification, and/or margins (at least one of the following): paragraphs indented, extra double-spaces, incorrect heading and/or signature line, other	Too many mistakes in spacing, justification, and/or margins (more than one of the following): paragraphs indented, extra double-spaces, incorrect heading and/or signature line, other
Grammar/ Punctuation	Minimal errors	Some errors	Egregious errors that interfere with meaning
Comments:			

Edna Pontellier

379 Awakening Lane

New Orleans, LA 17325

This sample letter is an amalgamation of a variety of past student letters. Since opportunities for events, speakers, and presentations vary from semester to semester, a model that is not necessarily based on the same speaker is actually more helpful for the students since they are more inclined to use it as a guide rather than rely on it as a blueprint.

April 15, 2011

Mr. John Smith

Liberal Arts College

188 Anywhere Ave.

Somewhere, NY 10128

Dear Mr. Smith:

I attended your presentation on African Drumming at the Celebration of Multicultural Arts Festival on Wednesday, April 11th. Your presentation was so interesting and I enjoyed learning about the origin of the drum. Thank you very much for the presentation.

I had not realized that the drum is created by using the hollow trunk of a tree, and I was fascinated by how complex the entire process of making a drum is—from worshiping the spirits that one believes to be in the tree, to cutting down the tree, and finally to carving it into the beautiful instrument that it eventually becomes. I also was interested in learning about the different techniques of playing the drums, such as signature drumming, and the dancing styles and speech mode that went along with the drumming. This combination of techniques and styles seems quite complicated; yet, when I asked you if musical training was a prerequisite for playing the drums, you said no knowledge of music was necessary.

Because this style of drumming originated in Africa and is part of the native culture, is it ingrained in the indigenous groups from a young age or do they still need to be taught just like someone in another country who would like to learn how to play them? For example, you mentioned that the playing of these drums is a form of religion to the African tribes. Does this mean that the knowledge of how to play the drums is something that comes naturally for those who grow up around it? Or would teaching still be necessary for the correct technique and style?

Thank you very much for your time. I look forward to learning more about the drums and possibly taking your course offered next semester!

Sincerely yours,

Edna Pontellier

Assignment 2: Argumentative Essay

ENG101: Composition

Writing Assignment: Argumentative Essay

Purpose of the assignment:

1. To demonstrate your ability to create and support a strong thesis statement
2. To demonstrate critical thinking skills by engaging with another point of view
3. To create paragraphs that are coherent and unified around one main point and that use effective transitions
4. To integrate at least one quote effectively and cite it correctly
5. To understand the process of revision (through a substantial revision!)

The purpose of the assignment is clearly stated for the student. She knows what she should focus on for this particular writing endeavor.

Requirements:

1. Minimum of three pages
2. Double-spaced, with 1″ margins, typed in Times New Roman, size 12 font
3. Formatted correctly (see **EW** page 410 for a sample MLA formatted essay), including a works-cited page

Requirements are clarified

Prompt:

You have read John Taylor Gatto's argument "Against School," where Gatto claims that formal schooling does not necessarily have the students' best interests in mind and, in fact, does them a disservice by *limiting* instead of strengthening their critical thinking skills. You have also discussed Billy Collins's poem "The History Teacher," where the teacher teaches in such a way that students learn only what he deems is safe for them to know. We have also examined our school's mission statement and discussed the inherent values and how they are being facilitated through your courses and curriculum. Write a paper in which you answer the following question: do American students need formal schooling?

The prompt reminds students of the discussions that have occurred in class to help them make connections, and the question itself is framed in such a way that a direct answer automatically generates an arguable thesis.

Before you approach this question, brainstorm the following:

How do you define education versus school (both informal and formal)?

How does your definition compare to or contrast with Gatto's definitions?

How do you know when you are learning?

In terms of your education, what expectations do you have of your instructors? Of yourself?

Do you take responsibility for your own education?

Providing some brainstorming questions to do outside of class is another form of scaffolding.

Due dates:

Monday:	In-class brainstorming; small-group work
Wednesday:	Choosing appropriate quotes for your points and counterpoints; quote integration/citation (Review **EW** pages 180–88 before class!)
Monday:	First (complete) draft for peer review; bring three focused questions you'd like your peers to address about your draft
Wednesday:	Revised draft, accompanied by (1) your original draft, and (2) a cover paragraph commenting on what you think the strongest area of your paper is and why

Note the way in which both scaffolding and sequencing are laid out in this assignment: this provides support for the student as well as helping to reduce plagiarism.

Other resources:

Review the basic tenets of constructing an argument on pages 126–40 in **EW**. And please feel free to use the writing center, the online tutoring lab, and/or make an appointment with me at any point during your writing process!

Listing extra resources is another form of scaffolding.

Evaluation:

Your paper will be evaluated according to the following rubric:

Objectives and Requirements	Strong	Okay	Needs Work	Comments
Thesis				
Support and development of thesis (sufficient details and examples)				
Organization and Structure: unified, cohesive paragraphs with effective use of transitions				
Effective engagement with another perspective (shows insight and grappling with topic)				

A rubric is one way to communicate to the students what is expected in the assignment; these criteria match the purpose of the assignment. This particular rubric provides more feedback rather than a grade since it is being used in a portfolio-based course where the student will be expected to revise the paper once again.

Evidence of substantive revision (not merely editing or surface changes)				
Effective and correct quote integration and citation				
Works Cited				
Minimal sentence-level errors				
Other comments:				

Assignment Template

First-Year Writing: An Assignment Template

Your assignment sheet should contain some or all of the following information. Instructors will vary on the length and level of detail they provide, depending on what best meets student needs.

Title of Assignment: _____

Draft Due Date: _____

Revision Due Date: _____

Conference Times: _____

Peer Review Dates: _____

Background/purpose of assignment

Here provide an overview of the assignment's purpose and objectives, detailing any key concepts, terms, and strategies you have discussed in class and explaining how students might use them in responding to the assignment.

Logistics

Here give requirements including length, format, and discussion of audience.

Drafting/writing process

Here list suggestions about how students might go about planning, researching, and writing the first draft of the assignment. Some instructors include a short bulleted list of ideas; others include a page-long narrative on possible steps and resources.

Expectations/revision/the final essay

Here you can list the elements required for final drafts and a summary/review of your evaluation criteria, which you should have handed out separately early on in the quarter or for each assignment. While not all instructors include such a section, it can be helpful to students in some form—especially if you spend time in class highlighting your expectations for the final essay!

Sample Syllabi

Syllabus 1: *The St. Martin's Handbook*

This syllabus outlines an introductory course in expository writing. Students learn to draft, revise, and edit short papers in which they state and develop a thesis. The reader in the course, *The Presence of Others*, is a collection designed to provoke thinking about a range of contemporary concerns. Students thus practice critical reading in close conjunction with writing, using selections from the reader—along with their own ideas and experiences—to generate material for papers.

Students write a total of six short papers: an in-class diagnostic sample at the beginning of the term, four out-of-class essays, and a final exam. Instructors may also want to include informal writing activities, such as exercises and responses to readings.

Books

Andrea A. Lunsford, *The St. Martin's Handbook*, 7th ed. (Bedford/St. Martin's, 2011) = *SMH*

Andrea A. Lunsford and John J. Ruszkiewicz, *The Presence of Others: Voices and Images That Call for Response*, 5th ed. (Bedford/St. Martin's, 2008) = *PO*

Schedule

Early in the term, students read the *Handbook* chapters about the larger elements of composition—invention and arrangement. As the term progresses, they study increasingly smaller matters of style, first the paragraph, then the sentence, and finally diction. On days when papers are collected and returned, the syllabus allows time for covering the "tools" of writing—grammar, punctuation, mechanics. Any *Handbook* assignments for these class meetings should be geared to the needs of students at that point in the course.

Week 1

1. **Paper 1 written in class** (diagnostic writing sample)
2. Introduction to the course; *SMH* Top Twenty and Chapter 1; *PO* Chapter 1 (reading and thinking critically)
3. Paper 1 returned and discussed; selection(s) from *PO*

Week 2

1. Paper 2 assigned; selection(s) from *PO*; *SMH* Chapter 2 (rhetorical situations)
2. Selection(s) from *PO*; *SMH* Chapter 2 (rhetorical situations continued)
3. Selection(s) from *PO*; *SMH* Chapter 3 (exploring, planning, and drafting)

→

Week 3

1. Working thesis and plan for Paper 2 due; workshop to review theses/plans
2. Workshop continued
3. Draft of Paper 2 due (two copies); peer-review workshop, with emphasis on thesis, organization, and development; *SMH* Chapter 4 (reviewing, revising, and editing)

Week 4

1. **Paper 2 due**; workshop—papers annotated, proofread, and discussed; bring *SMH* to class for review
2. Selection(s) from *PO*
3. Paper 3 assigned; selection(s) from *PO*

Week 5

1. Paper 2 returned and discussed; bring *SMH* to class for review
2. Selection(s) from *PO*
3. Selection(s) from *PO*; *SMH* Chapter 5 (developing paragraphs)

Week 6

1. Working thesis and plan for Paper 3 due; workshop to review theses/plans
2. Workshop continued; *SMH* 5f (opening and concluding paragraphs)
3. Draft of Paper 3 due; peer-review workshop, with special attention to introductions, conclusions, and body paragraphs

Week 7

1. **Paper 3 due**; workshop—papers annotated, proofread, and discussed; bring *SMH* to class for review
2. Selection(s) from *PO*
3. Paper 4 assigned; selection(s) from *PO*

Week 8

1. Paper 3 returned and discussed; bring *SMH* to class for review
2. Selection(s) from *PO*
3. Selection(s) from *PO*; *SMH* Chapter 40 (concise writing)

Week 9

1. Working thesis and plan for Paper 4 due; workshop to review theses/plans
2. *SMH* Chapter 42 (sentence variety)
3. Draft of Paper 4 due; peer-review workshop, with special attention to revising for effective and varied sentences

Week 10

1. **Paper 4 due**; workshop—papers annotated, proofread, and discussed; bring *SMH* to class for review

2. Selection(s) from *PO*

3. Paper 5 assigned; selection(s) from *PO*

Week 11

1. Paper 4 returned and discussed; bring *SMH* to class for review

2. Selection(s) from *PO*

3. Selection(s) from *PO*; *SMH* Chapter 43 (memorable prose)

Week 12

1. Selection(s) from *PO*

2. Selection(s) from *PO*; *SMH* Chapter 27 (word choice)

3. Working thesis and plan for Paper 5 due; workshop to review theses/plans

Week 13

1. Draft of Paper 5 due; peer-review workshop, with special attention to revising for memorable prose

2. Peer-review workshop continued, with special attention to revising for effective diction

3. **Paper 5 due**; workshop—papers annotated, proofread, and discussed; bring *SMH* to class for review

Week 14

1. Preparation for **final exam** (**Paper 6**)—an essay in which students assess their strengths and weaknesses as writers; review *SMH* Top Twenty and Chapter 1

2. Workshop—review of students' writing portfolios (all drafts and graded papers) in preparation for final exam

3. Paper 5 returned and discussed; review of portfolios continued

ENG101-20: Composition

YOUR COLLEGE NAME

FALL 2011

Meeting Times/Place: T/Th 8:30–9:50; W218 in Smith Hall
Instructor: Dr. Lisa Dresdner
Contact Information: Ldresdner@yourcollegename.edu or (xxx) xxx-xxxx
Office: W106, Smith Hall
Office Hours: M,T,W, and Th 10–12:00 PM and by appointment

Catalog description

This course develops students' abilities to write effective essays and to reason critically. A review of grammar and syntax, as needed, is included. The goals of unity, coherence, and logical development are pursued through practice in prewriting, writing, and revising techniques. Students learn various organizational patterns. Students will write and revise several essays.

(Prerequisites: Placement is determined by a college entrance exam, completion of ENG084 with a C minus or better, or by recommendation of the ESL faculty.)

Required texts and supplies

McQuade, Donald, and Robert Atwan. *The Writer's Presence: A Pool of Readings.* Boston: Bedford, 2006. **(WP)**

Lunsford, Andrea A. *The Everyday Writer.* 4th ed. Boston: Bedford/St. Martin's, 2009. **(EW)**

Handouts as needed and distributed

USB flash drive

2 folders: 1 for journals; 1 for drafts

Course learning outcomes:

I. Critical literacy

Upon successful completion of ENG101, students should be able to

1. support and develop a thesis-driven paper, using credible and adequate source material, in an essay more than three pages in length;

2. engage in a dialogue with a text, integrating their own ideas with those of others; and

3. know how to identify and evaluate sources as evidenced by creating an annotative and denotative bibliography (that is, explaining the reasons why sources are used and not used).

II. Process

Upon successful completion of ENG101, students should be able to

1. demonstrate understanding that writing is a process by creating a portfolio that includes a paper that has gone through the prewriting, drafting, revising, and editing stages;

2. practice reflection on their writing through a letter or essay that reflects on their growth and learning as a writer, with supportive evidence from their own papers.

III. Knowledge of conventions

On successful completion of ENG101, students should be able to

1. quote, paraphrase, and summarize a text effectively and correctly as evidenced with proper citation and documentation in a finished essay;

2. demonstrate understanding of academic writing conventions and make appropriate decisions about grammar, usage, punctuation, word choice, and style as evidenced through limited sentence-level errors in their final papers.

Grades

Your final grade for the course will be calculated in the following manner:

Final Portfolio	70%
Journals	15%
Participation/in-class work	15%

Throughout the semester, you will NOT receive grades on your writing assignments since they are works in progress. You will be given your essays back with comments and suggestions for revision, but there will not be a grade placed on the paper. Instead, your essays will be reviewed as part of a portfolio of your work at the end of the semester, and each paper included in the portfolio must have undergone significant revision. The goal here is not to grade you on your first attempt at writing, but, rather, to grade you based on how well you can revise, change, and grow as a writer.

In order to transfer ENG101 to another school, you must earn a C minus or better.

At midterm, your work will be assigned either a P (pass), a D (low pass), or an F (fail), depending on the quality of your writing and participation up to that point.

Class policies and procedures

Attendance policy

Prompt and regular attendance is vital for success. The discussions and in-class work are the means by which you will come to understand the concepts and objectives of this class. Additionally, we will start many classes with a writing exercise; therefore, I will start class on time! If you are more than fifteen minutes late to class, you will be counted as absent. The college Attendance Policy states that you may fail if you miss more than six classes! Thus, if you miss more than six classes after the first week, you will fail. At the very least, missing too many classes will adversely affect your grade.

If extenuating circumstances arise at any point during the semester, please contact me as soon as possible. We will discuss what action to take concerning your work.

I also realize that life gets in the way of school sometimes, so I won't be surprised if you miss a class or two. *Remember, though, that you are responsible for what goes on in a class you have missed, and you should find out what went on in your absence.* To that end, you might want to take down several of your peers' phone numbers, or you may always stop by or call me. If you do miss a class, please do not ask me if you "missed anything important." Everything we do in class is important!

Late assignment policy

All assignments are due when I collect them at the beginning of a class period on its due date as noted in the syllabus or as we will have discussed in class. Equipment failure of any kind will not constitute a valid excuse for not handing in an assignment. If an assignment is done during class—usually within the first fifteen minutes—and you are absent or tardy, you will not be able to make up that assignment or be given extra time. If you have an emergency, please contact me within twenty-four hours of the missed class to determine if alternative arrangements can be made.

Academic dishonesty

Cheating in any form is a serious offense, and as defined by the Student Handbook, academic dishonesty includes but is not limited to the following:

1. cheating on examinations and/or quizzes;
2. plagiarizing, including the submission of others' ideas or papers (whether purchased, borrowed, or otherwise obtained) as one's own work.

Penalties for academic dishonesty in my class are as follows: in the first instance, the assignment fails and you do not have the opportunity to make it up. In the second instance, you fail the class. I urge you to ask me any questions if you are uncertain about whether what you are writing is an offense of academic dishonesty.

Academic writing

I will not accept any draft that does not conform to the university conventions of academic writing.

Cell phones, iPods, and any other distracting electronic devices

Turn them off! Let's respect each other by focusing on the time we spend together in class.

Portfolio

To complete ENG101 successfully, you must submit a passing portfolio of writing at the end of the semester. This portfolio will be selected from assignments completed and revised during the semester and will also include a reflective cover letter addressing the contents of your portfolio. Including the cover letter, the portfolio must contain fifteen full pages of typed, double-spaced writing of your final copies.

Because the writing is viewed as a process in ENG101, you are expected to make sure that all the papers submitted in the portfolio have undergone substantial revision and editing. You will be including at least one paper that shows the multiple drafts with my comments as evidence of the revisions you have made during the writing process. Remember: you are being graded not just on the quality of your writing but also on your ability to revise and grow as a writer.

The portfolio will be read and assessed by at least two people: me and another faculty member from the English Department. The outside reader will assign one of three grades: P for Pass, P minus for low pass, or NP for not passing. I will assign the letter grade to the portfolio. If your portfolio receives a grade of NP from the outside reader, the portfolio will fail. Your portfolio must pass the assessment for you to pass the course.

As the semester continues, I will give you more information on how to assemble your portfolio. For now, keep in mind that you should be saving all work done in this class for further use.

Revision

Because we often learn much about our own writing by revising it, and because I embrace the philosophy that writing is a process, revision exercises are built into our class schedule.

I also encourage and expect you to revise papers before you submit them to me the first time. Up to three weeks after receiving back a reviewed paper, you may submit a revision of it for an additional critique by me. <u>When submitting a revision, you must hand in the original draft with my comments or I will not critique it.</u> I will not critique revisions that are handed in after this three-week period. However, if at any point during the semester you would like additional comments on a draft, please feel free to set up an appointment with me. Bear in mind that as the end of the semester nears, these appointment times fill up very quickly.

Additionally, after I have critiqued and commented on your portfolio papers, you must revise them once again before submitting them in your portfolio.

Accommodations

Students with disabilities who anticipate the need for accommodations should call the Disabilities Office at XXX–XXXX or go to W209. If you are in need of accommodation for any type of documented disability, please feel free to discuss this need with me *during the first two weeks of class.*

Resources

You have a lot of resources to help you with your college classes! These include the following:
- **Me!** *Make appointments; speak with me after class; use me as much as you want!*
- **Writing Center** (times TBA)
- **E-tutoring:** You can log onto www.etutoring.org at anytime during the semester and submit a paper for review and critique by an outside reader, usually one who is a professor or who has an advanced degree.
- **Tutoring Center** (located on the first floor in the B wing of the West Campus)
- **ESL Tutoring** (if you are a former ESL student)

Syllabus modification

Be prepared throughout the semester to have the syllabus modified to some extent.

A final note

I look forward to watching you grow as a writer. Because I put a lot of energy and effort into teaching, I expect you to do the same with learning. During class I will respect your ideas and expect you to respect mine. I work hard to promote your development so that you are proud of your work and have a sense of accomplishment when you have completed this course. Let's enjoy our time together and learn from each other!

I assume that your presence in class indicates your willingness to abide by these policies.

• •

Course Withdrawal Deadlines: November 18th is the LAST DAY TO WITHDRAW FROM A COURSE WITHOUT EXTENUATING CIRCUMSTANCES. After this date a student may submit a written petition to the Academic Dean to withdraw from a course due to extenuating circumstances. The petition form can be obtained from the Dean's Office. If the petition is approved by the Academic Dean, a grade of "W" will appear on your transcript.

ENG101-20 Schedule of Classes and Assignments

Monday	**Week 1: Introduction to ENG101** • Introductions • Go over syllabus • Diagnostic writing
Wednesday	**Writing Triad, Audience, and Purpose** • Homework: email assignment, due to me by Friday at noon! • *The Everyday Writer* (**EW**): discuss 43–48 (writing situation) and 15–16 (email) • Paper assignment #1: first draft due Wednesday, week 3

Monday	**Week 2: Writing Process** • Return emails; discuss them • **EW**: discuss 52–57; In-class writing—brainstorming techniques • *The Writer's Presence* (**WP**): read Langston Hughes, 145–46 ("How to Be a Bad Writer [in Ten Easy Lessons]") and Stephen King, 440–46 ("Everything You Need to Know about Writing Successfully—in Ten Minutes") • Journal #1: engage in a dialogue with the text by integrating your ideas with the author's: copy a statement you find important or provocative in one of the readings in **WP** and respond as if you are actually talking to the author. (Be aware of your tone.)
Wednesday	**Purpose/Audience/Tone** Discuss Hughes and King essays in terms of purpose, audience, and tone. Identify words that demonstrate tone. How would you change the tone of your response?

Monday	**Week 3: Thesis Statement** • **EW**: 58–60 • **WP**: Katha Pollitt, 522–24 ("Why Boys Don't Play with Dolls") and Scott Russell Sanders, 828–32 ("The Men We Carry in Our Minds") • Small-group work: thesis identification and supporting details in **WP** essays and in your own essay: use **EW** (7b) game plan, page 59
Wednesday	• **Peer Review Workshop** • **DUE**: draft of paper #1 • **EW**: be familiar with pages 82–86 and 91–94 • **EW**: 98–99 review sample student revision Journal #2: summarize the feedback you received from your group of peers about your essay and explain two significant changes you will make in your revision and why.

Monday	**Week 4: Effective Paragraphs: Unity and Coherence** • **EW**: 68–70 and 77–80 (be familiar with this section on paragraphs—we'll refer to it often) "Show vs. Tell" and "Ladder of Abstraction": in-class writing **DUE**: revised paper #1 • **WP**: Amy Cunningham, 324–30 ("Why Women Smile") • Assign paper #2, draft due Wednesday, week 5 • Journal #3: write one page about an experience when you have been stereotyped based on your gender. What are your observations of this stereotype and what have been the consequences for you?
Wednesday	**Introductions and Conclusions** • Discuss **EW**: 80–81 (8f) • **WP**: Sherry Turkle, 564–69 ("How Computers Change the Way We Think") and Charles McGrath, 473–75 ("The Pleasures of the Text") • Journal #4: identify the main point in either McGrath's or Turkle's essay and write a one-page response to it, using your own experience for support. Details!

Monday	**Week 5: Quote Integration** • **EW**: 180–88 • In-class work: practice integrating/citing quotes for paper #2 • Return Paper #1; discuss
Wednesday	**Peer Review Workshop** • **DUE**: draft Paper #2 • Journal #5: read through the comments on your first paper and think about how the feedback from the peer-review workshop today connects to those comments. Write one page about what you are learning about your writing so far.

Monday	**Week 6: Research!** • **EW: 149–54** • **DUE**: revised paper #2 • **Assign Research Paper (in steps)**
Wednesday	**Research Paper: Choosing the Topic; Developing the Question** • **Journal #6:** write 1–2 pages on a topic about which you feel some passion; explore why you feel so strongly about it, what you know about it, and what questions you have about it. • Be prepared to share this journal in class today for small-group work.

Monday	**Week 7: Meet in the Library at Our Regular Class Time** • **Research Paper:** finding and evaluating sources • **EW**: 154–56 and 169–72
Wednesday	**Summary/Paraphrase: Review** • **EW**: 180–88 • Practice summary and paraphrase in class

Monday	**Week 8: Argument**
	• **EW**: 123–40; pay close attention to the sample student writing on pages 123–25
	• **WP**: Nora Ephron, 676–82 ("The Boston Photographs")
	• Discuss Ephron's essay and analyze how she makes her argument
	• **DUE**: summary of one article you will use in your research paper
Wednesday	**Research Paper: Small-Group Work**
	• **DUE**: working thesis for your research paper
	• **Journal #7**: write a letter to your best friend explaining your research project and what you have discovered so far

Monday	**Week 9: Argument (Reconsidered)**
	• **WP**: Peter Singer, 849–55 ("The Singer Solution to World Poverty")
	• Analyze and discuss how Singer makes his argument.
	• **DUE**: bibliographic information on one article you will not use and a fully developed paragraph explaining why not
Wednesday	**Speaker Event**
	• Attendance is mandatory: take notes! Your letter assignment is directly linked to this event.
	• **Assignment**: letter, due Wednesday, week 10
	• **Journal #8**: Review the drafts of your papers and your journal entries so far; think about what you have learned so far this semester and how your writing has progressed. Write one page about your growth as a writer, referring to specific examples from your writing or lessons you've learned.

Monday	**Week 10: Formatting a Letter**
	• Discuss speaker and letter requirements; work in class on letter
	• **EW**: 556
	• **DUE**: draft of research paper (I will take these home and comment on them.)
Wednesday	**Letter: Tone/Purpose/Audience**
	• Work in class on letter
	• **DUE**: letter assignment
	• **Assignment**: Paper #4, draft due Wednesday, week 11

Monday	**Week 11: In-Class Work on Paper #4**
Wednesday	**Peer Review**
	DUE: draft of Paper #4
	Return letter assignment

Monday	**Week 12: Return Research Papers for Revision** Discuss revision strategies for research papers **DUE**: revised Paper #4
Wednesday	**Reflective Cover Letter** **EW**: 99–102

Monday	**Week 13: Portfolio Preparation Workshop** Return Paper #4
Wednesday	**Portfolio Preparation Workshop**

Monday	**Week 14: Portfolio Preparation Workshop**
Wednesday	**Portfolio Preparation Workshop**

Syllabus 3: *EasyWriter*

This syllabus outlines a course in writing about literature. Such courses are typically offered as the second half of a two-part composition sequence, taken after students have completed an earlier course in expository writing. In the version that follows, students develop critical reading skills, write literary analyses, and use secondary sources to support their ideas. They learn to quote, summarize, and paraphrase, demonstrating these skills in short essays and in a longer documented paper. The reader in the course—*Literature: The Human Experience*—is organized thematically and includes works in four genres (fiction, poetry, drama, and the essay).

Students write three short papers, a longer research paper, and, near the end of the term, an in-class essay. This last piece helps prepare them for the final exam, an additional in-class essay. Instructors may also want to add informal writing assignments, such as entries in a reading journal.

Books

Andrea A. Lunsford, *EasyWriter*, 4th ed. (Bedford/St. Martin's, 2010) = *EZ*

Richard Abcarian and Marvin Klotz, *Literature: The Human Experience*, 10th ed. (Bedford/St. Martin's, 2010) = *L*

Schedule

In the early part of the course, *EasyWriter* assignments provide an overview of the writing process and teach students about literary analysis. Later, students make extensive use of the chapters on doing research and documentation. They also bring *EasyWriter* to class for review on days when papers are collected and returned. And throughout the term, they consult the book on their own as a tool for drafting and revising their papers.

Week 1

1. Introduction to the course: analytical reading and writing
2. *L* 3–6, and *EZ* 5b (reading and writing in the humanities); story selected from *L*
3. *L* 11–19; poem selected from *L*

Week 2

1. Paper 1 assigned (500-word literary analysis with citations from text); *EZ* Chapter 2 (review of the writing process: exploring, planning, and drafting); *L* 73–77 (preliminary information about quoting and documenting)
2. Selection(s) from *L*
3. Selection(s) from *L*

Week 3

1. Working thesis and plan for Paper 1 due; workshop to review theses/ plans; *EZ* 2f–2h (review of the writing process: reviewing, revising, and editing)
2. Draft of Paper 1 due; peer-review workshop
3. **Paper 1 due**; workshop—papers proofread and discussed; bring *EZ* to class; selection(s) from *L*

Week 4

1. Selection(s) from *L*

2. Paper 2 assigned (750-word literary analysis with citations from primary text and one secondary source); selection(s) from *L*

3. Paper 1 returned and discussed; bring *EZ* to class; selection from *L*

Week 5

1. Selection(s) from *L*; *EZ* 40a–b (integrating sources: quotations, paraphrases, summaries, and visuals)

2. Working thesis and plan for Paper 2 due; workshop to review theses/ plans; integrating sources continued

3. Draft of Paper 2 due; peer-review workshop

Week 6

1. **Paper 2 due**; workshop—papers proofread and discussed; bring *EZ* to class; Paper 3 assigned (750-word literary analysis with citations from primary text and minimum of two secondary sources)

2. Selection(s) from *L*

3. Selection(s) from *L*

Week 7

1. Paper 2 returned and discussed; bring *EZ* to class; thesis and plan for Paper 3 due; workshop to review theses/plans

2. *EZ* Chapter 39 (evaluating sources), Chapter 40 (integrating sources), and Chapter 42 (MLA style)

3. Draft of Paper 3 due; peer-review workshop

Week 8

1. Paper 4 assigned (1,500-word literary analysis with citations from primary text[s] and minimum of five secondary sources); writing from sources continued

2. **Paper 3 due**; workshop—papers proofread and discussed; bring *EZ* to class

3. *EZ* Chapter 41 (writing a research project)

Week 9

1. Working thesis and plan for Paper 4 due; workshop to review theses/ plans

2. Paper 3 returned and discussed; bring *EZ* to class; selection(s) from *L*

3. Selection(s) from *L*

Week 10

1. Review material from *EZ* Chapters 38–42 (research and documentation)

2. Draft of Paper 4 due; peer-review workshop

3. Peer-review workshop continued

Week 11

1. Peer-review workshop continued

2. **Paper 4 due**; workshop—papers proofread and discussed; bring *EZ* to class

3. Selection(s) from *L*

Week 12

1. Selection(s) from *L*
2. Selection(s) from *L*
3. Preparation for Paper 5 (500-word in-class literary analysis)

Week 13

1. Paper 4 returned and discussed; bring *EZ* to class; preparation for Paper 5 continued
2. **Paper 5 drafted in class**
3. Paper 5 revised and edited in class

Week 14

1. Selection(s) from *L* for use in **final exam**—a 500-word in-class essay
2. Selection(s) from *L*; preparation for final exam continued
3. Paper 5 returned and discussed; bring *EZ* to class

Responding to Student Writing

Nothing creates more anxiety and panic than that moment when a composition instructor faces the first overwhelming pile of papers that is waiting to be read and evaluated. Unless, of course, it is the anxiety and panic that students experience when they get a paper returned, especially if it is covered in red ink.

To avoid, or at least reduce, the dread faced by both the instructor and the student in what is perhaps one of the most important parts of teaching writing—*responding to the writer*—it is helpful to follow a few basic strategies.

Know Your Purposes in Responding

Two key factors determine the types of comments you will make and the kinds of issues you will address in your response to students' writing:

1. At what point are the students in the writing process?
2. At what level of writing are the students?

Your comments on an *initial* draft with *novice* writers will differ from comments on a *second* or *third* draft with more *experienced* writers. Earlier drafts, as you might imagine, usually require comments that are more **global**, or are macro-level in nature—responding to the essay as a whole; whereas later drafts lend themselves to comments regarding more **local**, or micro-level issues, responding on the sentence level. Likewise, a novice writer, who is likely less in control of her topic and approach, will require feedback that might help her articulate what and how she is thinking through a subject; whereas a more experienced writer, who has a stronger grasp of her argument, may require feedback that helps her organize her attempts at a synthesis of several ideas.

Responding to students' writing is another opportunity to teach a lesson, but students can learn only a few lessons at a time. Try to teach them too much at once and you run the risk of overwhelming them with information, which often results in paralysis rather than action. Thus, when considering your purpose in providing feedback, ask yourself what two (or three at the most) main lessons you want your students to take away. What do you want the student to do with the information you are providing in the comments? Will the student know how to improve his paper?

Global or macro-level issues—a focus on content and structural areas:

- strong thesis
- argument that is sufficiently developed
- clear points that are adequately supported with acceptable evidence
- logical and coherent organization of ideas
- unified paragraphs
- overall draft meets the rhetorical demands of the assignment

Local or micro-level issues—a focus on paragraph, sentence, or word-choice areas:

- transitions between paragraphs and/or sentences
- grammar, punctuation, and spelling
- word choice or stylistic concerns
- proofreading mistakes

Types of Comments

Facilitative Comments: These comments facilitate the learning process by engaging the writer in a dialogue. Think of your comments as another kind of lesson for the student: What do you want to teach the student through your comments? What information do you want the student to come away with after reading your comments and then, importantly, do with what she has learned from them?

Try to engage the writer by asking questions, and in so doing demonstrate respect for the writer's authority and his attempts to say something. Posing questions also helps you avoid falling into the habit of commenting only on what is wrong or constantly phrasing comments in a negative way. Thus, instead of writing, "This point does not relate to your larger argument," ask "How does this point relate to your larger argument?" Sometimes you might find it necessary to ask a series of questions: "What is the main point in this paragraph? Does every sentence relate to that point? Should some of these points be developed more fully in their own paragraph?" Remember, too, that if the writing seems unorganized or confused it may not be because the writer was hasty or didn't care but, rather, that she is confused herself in her thinking about the topic. Try posing questions that help her to clarify her meaning: "Are you trying to argue that the purpose of movies is to entertain by both horrifying and engendering happiness in audiences?"

Too many questions, though, can overwhelm a student, who may not know where to start the revision process; and it is just as important and useful to point out things that are particularly well done and suggest that the student do more of that. Did the student use detail or examples in an effective way? Or utilize an especially effective transition? Or construct some particularly nice phrasing? Let him know what he is doing well to encourage and nurture his skill and confidence.

Directive Comments: As the name suggests, these comments direct the student to revise or change something in a specific way. To be most effective, though, they should include an explanation of *why* the change will strengthen the writing. For example, the comment "Move this paragraph to the beginning of your paper" lets the student know what he needs to do, but it doesn't teach him anything. Additionally, the imperative "move" may sound to the student as though the instructor is taking control of her writing, which she may resist. A more effective way to direct students in their revision process would be to frame your comment as a suggestion followed by an explanation: "If you move this paragraph to the beginning of your paper you'll build a stronger framework for your argument and the supporting details will be more effective because they'll have some context." This type of specificity and explanation also provides the student with transferable information that she can use in future writing endeavors.

Even more effective is when a directive comment is combined with a facilitative one. For example:

> These two sentences don't seem to relate to the larger point you are making in this paragraph and should be moved or omitted. Did you want to shift the focus here? Or can you see where you might use them more effectively in your paper and develop them more fully on their own?

Evaluative Comments: These are often written as end comments on a final draft. While they are in some instances considered the *justification* for a grade, they should instead be considered as a way to respond to the essay as a whole, commenting on the argument and its presentation and development, perhaps adding a suggestion for the writer to consider in the next assignment. Again, what makes these types of comments most beneficial to a student is their specificity: vague or general phrasings such as "Good job!" or "Nice work!" don't really offer much useful information to the student. Respond honestly, be positive in your initial statement, and relate your comments to the learning outcomes of the assignment.

Know Your Role as a Responder

When you read and respond to your students, being aware of the multiple roles you take will help you frame your feedback:

As a reader: This is probably your most important role, because in this capacity you demonstrate to your student writers that you take what they are saying seriously. Writing is often an act of vulnerability: beginning writers especially are uncertain about the value of what they have to say. But when a student sees that you care what he has to say, he will start to care more, too, about what and how he is saying things. When you respond as a reader, you are validating the significance of the content of the paper, which helps the student know that he is in a conversation with a reader.

As a teacher: In this role, you alternate between being a coach and being an evaluator. While in the evaluator role you need to assess the writing and to show the student where and how to improve, you also need to engage the strategies of a good coach by encouraging, nurturing, and celebrating the good stuff! Striking a balance between the two is imperative in creating the optimum conditions for students to learn what they need to do to improve their writing and to gain the confidence to do so.

As an editor: Most composition instructors simply can't help reading and responding from this position; however, this is actually the *least* important of the roles. Your job is not to change a student's writing style; nor is it to mark or correct all sentence-level errors. In fact, marking too many sentence-level errors, or marking any of them too soon, can have the opposite effect from what you want: either the student will correct only those errors (after all, they are easy to correct since they've been marked) but will not have learned anything in the process, or the student will be so overwhelmed by all the markings that she will do nothing. Take care not to let the editor get in the way of the reader or the teacher.

Understand the Student's Perspective

Most students arrive at college expecting to see a grade at the end of a paper, and instructor comments—whether written in the margins or as end comments—can be so overwhelming that students simply do not read them. They often assume that the comments are negative, and they do not understand the point of reading them.

Sometimes what is most obvious to you is not at all clear to the student. For example, one instructor wrote next to a paragraph the following comment: "This paragraph jumps from point to point." In the instructor's mind, she was making a specific observation that would let the student know that he needs to write a paragraph that is unified around only one point. However, the simple observation that the paragraph jumps from point to point tells the writer nothing; in fact, he may not even know whether that is a positive or a negative comment. Similarly, a series of abbreviations written in the margins, such as "awk," "frag," "run-on," or the ubiquitous "?" (sometimes doubled or tripled for apparent emphasis—"???"), serve only to frustrate the student to the point of ignoring the marks. And really, if we are expecting students to be aware of audience and purpose for clarity of writing, we should be doing the same with our comments. When the student is at a point in the writing process that micro-level comments are helpful, be sure that you have explained what your editorial abbreviations mean, and take care to point students to sections in the handbook that will help them correct and learn from their errors.

Since your feedback is, in effect, engaging the student writer in a conversation, before students hand in their papers have them write a paragraph or two that addresses specific questions, such as what they see as their strongest area of writing, what parts they are the least or most satisfied with, and what questions they have about particular parts of their papers. You might also have them pose two to three explicit questions they have about their papers. This student perspective will help to guide you in your own comments and allow you to begin a dialogue with the student.

While writing comments is laborious and time-intensive work, when we take care to construct them in such a way that students know what they mean and what to do with them, then we are providing a more effective learning environment.

The Realities of the Paper Load

Twenty minutes seems to be the mythical amount of time that one "should" spend reading and responding to each student paper, although that twenty minutes does not account for the stage, length, or complexity of the paper *or* for the experience of the instructor, all of which affect how much time you'll spend with your students' papers. And the reality is that you will never be able to spend the amount of time you would *like* to on each paper. There are, however, several strategies that will help to make your approach to papers both more effective and more efficient.

First, review your assignment. Remind yourself what prompt you asked your students to respond to and what objectives they are supposed to meet so that you have a better idea of what you will be reading and how you might respond.

Second, put your pen or pencil away. This is by far the biggest challenge for all composition instructors, because most of us find the acts of reading, thinking, and writing inseparable. Moreover, every little error in grammar or punctuation will jump out of the sentence and beg to be circled or underlined or corrected; but you must resist doing so, because what you want to read for initially is the main point of the paper. If you get caught up in the sentence-level issues, you will miss the bigger picture. And those micro-level errors will change and possibly even disappear on their own as students develop their writing skills by the time the second or third draft gets written. Remember that writing is a recursive act, so read quickly and holistically the first time.

Third, read several batches of papers at once. By doing so you get a sense of common issues that you can address in a single handout or lesson to the entire class. Are the majority of your students struggling with articulating a clear thesis statement? transitions between paragraphs? specific patterns of grammar and punctuation errors? Addressing these kinds of issues all at once saves you from having to write the same type of comment on each paper individually.

Fourth, remember the focus and purpose of your feedback. If, however, sentence-level errors are egregious enough to interfere with understanding, then mark only one or two paragraphs and comment about the pattern(s) of errors you notice, directing students to resources to help them correct and learn from their mistakes. As with your other comments, though, students can learn only a few lessons at a time; so rather than mark every single error even in the one to two paragraphs, choose the two or three types of errors that you want the student to work on for the next paper.

Finally, try typing your comments. If you have your students hand in their papers by hard copy rather than through a course management system or by email (at which point you can use word-tracking for your comments), keeping your hands away from the paper and typing your comments accomplishes two things: first, most people can type faster than they can write by hand, so you can actually end up writing more substantial comments; and, second, keeping your hands away from the paper allows you to see and read it more comprehensively.

Utilize Other Types of Feedback

The paper load in a composition classroom can also be made more manageable by employing other strategies that, simultaneously, provide additional learning opportunities.

Rubrics

Of all the tools at an instructor's disposal, rubrics are perhaps the least understood and the most contentious. Those who argue against using them believe that they dehumanize the student by using a "machine" rather than a "human" response; that they are too limiting; or that they do not provide the individualized, hands-on feedback that can be so effective for students.

Yet rubrics are an extremely effective way to clarify expectations for students and, in so doing, demystify the writing process. They can, indeed, take the "guesswork" out of the writing process: when given to students along with the assignment, rubrics let them know what components will be evaluated in the paper and what they should focus on as they revise and build their skills.

Creating an effective rubric is not difficult, but there are so many resources in print and online that you should not have to start from scratch. Find one that is as close to your situational needs as possible, and then adapt it. The basic components include the following:

- determining the criteria you want to evaluate;
- limiting the number of criteria so that it is manageable (and no longer than one page);
- developing quality descriptions for each criterion and its levels;
- using clear, professional language;
- revising and refining: developing rubrics involves an iterative process; and
- providing models of finished assignments whenever possible.

Another idea is to consider having your students help to develop the rubric; doing so further emphasizes the lesson and helps to ensure understanding of expectations. Additionally, it gives students more reasons to buy into the process.

Individual Conferences

Setting aside extra office hours or, if your department allows, canceling a class to schedule individual ten- to fifteen-minute conferences will go a long way toward personalizing feedback for your students. You will find that you can talk through the issues in a paper and explain revision strategies more effectively in a ten-minute personal conference with a student than you can in writing. And the student almost always gets more out of a one-on-one conference with you. The value of personal conferencing cannot be overemphasized.

Peer Review

You don't always have to provide the feedback for your students yourself! In fact, teaching them effective ways to engage in peer review helps them on many levels: they begin to understand more fully that different audiences perceive things differently; they are exposed to different types of writing styles, which helps them develop their own; and the more they learn to engage and to respond to others' writing the more they will be able to read their own work critically with an eye toward revision.

There are, of course, many ways to approach peer review, and your handbook is an excellent resource for strategies, whether in pairs, small groups, or structured in varying degrees. But you want to be sure to model it for students and to emphasize that they are commenting on the writing, not the writer. Novice peer reviewers are often afraid that they will hurt the writers' feelings (or that their own feelings will be hurt). One way to demonstrate how to respond to the writing is to give them specific phrases as tools to get them started. Students need to practice peer review to become comfortable with it; and as they gain more confidence in themselves as writers, they will become more secure in their ability to comment on others' writing.

Student Reflection

Students' deepest learning occurs in the act of reflecting, so the more opportunities you can provide for them to engage in this practice, the better. The act of reflection serves as a site of inquiry into students' own learning processes: it prompts them to link new knowledge to prior knowledge; helps them make connections both to earlier work and to work in other courses or in their everyday lives; helps them apply new knowledge and skills in relevant ways; and, importantly, helps them understand their own learning strategies.

But many students are not used to reflection and cannot simply "reflect on command." Therefore, you need to set up specific tasks, often with explicit questions, to guide them through this process. Students might, for example, summarize your feedback and explain what they plan to do in their revisions. They might follow up this activity with a cover letter or even just a paragraph explaining what they did differently in the revision and how that revision made the paper stronger and/or what they learned about themselves as a writer in the process. If you are using a portfolio process for the course, they can refer to the reflective activities you ask them to do throughout the semester to write a more comprehensive cover letter for their entire portfolio.

Providing a list of questions that students can consider in their reflection will assist them in writing it, though you want to emphasize that the questions should simply be a way to get them started on their way to writing a reflective essay or cover letter.

1. What do you notice when you look at your earlier work?
2. How do you think your writing has changed?
3. What do you know about your writing now that you didn't before?
4. What do you understand about writing as a process?
5. What does that process look like for you? Describe it in as much detail as possible.

6. What kinds of revisions did you make on your papers?

7. How did you decide what to revise? What are some examples of changes you made?

8. How did those changes affect your final draft?

9. What kinds of weaknesses in your writing have you learned to identify?

10. How do you strengthen those areas?

11. What are some examples of particularly strong areas of your writing?

12. What have you learned about yourself as a writer?

Students learn by means of their own engaged scholarship, and maintaining a record of their growth as writers and learners makes student learning more visible, which, in turn, increases their critical thinking skills.

Using a Handbook

By Michael Hennessy, Texas State University

Some books are to be tasted, others to be swallowed, and some few to be chewed and digested; that is, some books are to be read only in parts; others to be read, but not curiously; and some few to be read wholly and with diligence and attention.

–Francis Bacon, "Of Studies"

A handbook for college writers—a category that includes *The St. Martin's Handbook, The Everyday Writer,* and *EasyWriter*—slips somewhat uneasily between Bacon's categories. Most of us would agree that such a book is primarily "to be tasted," to be read "in parts," rather than "swallowed" or "chewed and digested." Handbooks are essentially reference works, books we more often "consult" than read in long stretches. But this statement belies the fact that many of us own an old handbook, perhaps from our college days or earlier, that looks very much "chewed and digested" from repeated use. Over the years, we may have read the book "wholly and with diligence and attention": we know it inside out. And while we may ask our students to read parts of their handbooks "not curiously"—that is, quickly rather than carefully—there are other parts we want them to read and read again with great "diligence and attention."

This discussion suggests, perhaps, that a contemporary writing handbook is actually several books in one—a text we use in different ways at different times, a book whose function varies from teacher to teacher, course to course, and student to student. Any book in a composition class, of course, can vary in function depending on the pedagogical preferences of the instructor or the focus of the class. But handbooks are especially adaptable because of their encyclopedic qualities: they bring together large amounts of material, ranging from information about the recursive nature of the writing process and the qualities of memorable prose to minutiae about the placement of footnote numbers. Handbooks include an ambitious and—for some students—baffling array of grammatical rules, sample papers, charts, lists, checklists, style sheets, glossaries, and exercises—a compendium of information not designed for start-to-finish reading.

Because handbooks are by nature highly adaptable, instructors employ them in myriad ways. Some use a handbook as the backbone of a composition course, taking students systematically through large parts of the text; the work of the term is tied closely to the structure of the book itself. With *The St. Martin's Handbook*, for example, an instructor might begin at the beginning, moving from the larger elements of invention and arrangement toward smaller matters of style and convention. Another instructor, working from a different set of assumptions, might start with detailed in-class coverage of Chapters 29–33 on sentence grammar. At the other end of the spectrum are instructors whose classroom use of their handbook may consist of little more than holding the book up for students to see on the first day of the term. Such instructors may assign students to read some sections—perhaps the advice about the writing process. Beyond that, students are on their own with the book, using it as a reference tool, a guide for revising and editing their work. Between these extremes, of course, are many other points of balance.

In the next few pages—from my perspective as a composition director, supervisor of graduate assistants, and writing teacher—I offer a number of suggestions for using your handbook in a first-year composition course. I regularly conduct my classes as writing workshops in which students review one another's drafts and revise their work under my supervision. A handbook is therefore mainly a reference tool that students use on their own. I do make assignments from the book, but I rarely have time to "teach" them in class. And so, rather than attempting to offer a broad survey of the various ways the book might be used, I focus here on a few specific ways that instructors can help their students make the best use of the book as a writing guide and reference tool. My advice is aimed chiefly at new teachers of composition and at experienced teachers using one of the Lunsford handbooks for the first time.

Over the years, I have fielded dozens of questions about handbook use. "How should I use handbooks in class?" "How can I integrate the handbook with selections from the reader?" "Is there a way I can use it during writing workshops and peer-editing sessions?" "How can I encourage students to use it as they revise their own papers outside of class?" "Should I use the symbols at the back of the book when I grade papers?" "How can I get students to read the sections that I advise them to read when I comment on their drafts?" I have tried to keep these and other questions about handbooks in mind in offering the advice that follows.

Orienting Students to a Handbook

Whether you assign a Lunsford handbook as your primary classroom text or mainly as a guide for students to use on their own as they draft, revise, and edit their work, you will want to provide a thorough orientation to the book at the beginning of the term. Neglecting to do so can leave students frustrated in their efforts to understand the book's advice and to master its reference system. The handbook is a rich source of information and a powerful tool, but like any tool, its effectiveness depends on the skill of the person using it. A computer is worthless unless you know how to operate it. So, too, a writing handbook.

I am reminded of a junior transfer student who visited my office to discuss a paper she had written during her first term on campus. The paper had earned a low grade partly because of numerous surface errors. I asked the student if she owned a handbook in which she might review the problems identified in her paper. Her response was, "Yes, I still have the one I used in my freshman year, but I never have been able to figure out how to use it to fix problems in my writing." This anecdote goes to the heart of the matter: that many students find handbooks baffling, even mysterious texts, something altogether unfamiliar. Such students need *to be taught about the way a handbook works*: its organization, its language, its conventions. A text that seems perfectly transparent, logical, and "natural" to a writing teacher—a member of the discipline—may look strange, new, and "unnatural" to an uninitiated student.

One of the most essential things an instructor can do, then, is to demystify your handbook for students, to make them feel comfortable working with it, flipping through its pages, reading it, consulting it. Taking class time to describe, demonstrate, and practice the use of the book is always time well spent.

Even after students have grown relatively comfortable finding their way around in the book, they still may harbor misconceptions that you will want to address. A superficial familiarity with the text may lead them to conclude, for example, that good writing is essentially a matter of managing details—constructing error-free sentences, avoiding misspelled words, and putting commas where they belong. That students might develop such an impression is not altogether surprising: like most handbooks, the Lunsford handbooks have roughly as many pages about commas as they do about planning and drafting an essay, for example.

Students need to be told why this is so. They need to know that the author of the handbook, and the teacher using the book, do not necessarily endorse the idea that grammatical correctness takes precedence over the work of developing substantial, convincing ideas. It will be useful, then, to explain at the beginning of the term that the truly "basic" information in the book is located in the chapters on the writing process. You will want to tell students that the book emphasizes rhetorical choices rather than hard and fast rules. The details of style matter most during the revising and editing stages of the writing process, *after* the writer has dealt with larger issues of content, organization, and presentation. Students will be pleased to hear that they already follow, without thinking much about it, most of the "rules" and mechanical conventions that occupy a good portion of the book—and that those rules are there for reference, to be "read only in parts" rather than "wholly."

Here are three strategies that you might use at the beginning of the term to help orient yourself and your students to the book, to help students learn its conventions, and to undercut any faulty perceptions they may have about handbooks in general.

1. **If you are a new teacher, or if you are using this handbook for the first time, take time to familiarize yourself with the book**. Learn how it differs from other handbooks you have used. The preface describes the book's distinguishing features, explains how the book was developed, and spells out the author's assumptions about rhetoric, writing, reading, and the role of "correctness" in academic English. While the preface may not be of particular interest to students, it provides essential information for instructors planning to use the book. The more you know

about your handbook, the better equipped you will be to show students how it works.

2. **Give students a guided tour of the handbook**. Your doing so sends a clear message: that the book plays an essential role in the course you are teaching and that you expect students to consult it regularly. The tour need not take more than half a class period. Show students the book's endpapers, and explain how the information found there can be useful in tracking down important advice about writing. Review the table of contents to give students an overall sense of what the book includes. Finally, lead students through two chapters—one that gives advice about composing and one that deals with a particular grammatical or mechanical concern—highlighting various types of information and identifying useful features of the text.

3. **Make assignments from the handbook early in the term**. Even if you expect students to use the book mainly on their own as a reference guide, give at least one substantial reading assignment to the whole class during the first week of the course. A good choice is the chapter on expectations for academic writing. Take time to talk about the chapter, asking students to discuss what they learned and, in particular, to consider how the book's advice may help them as they draft and revise their papers later in the term. This sort of discussion can help establish a connection between the handbook and the rest of what students will do in the course.

After using *The St. Martin's Handbook* for a semester, one of my colleagues observed that she was starting to know the book well and was becoming increasingly "comfortable" with it. If we can likewise bring students to feel a certain level of "comfort" with their handbooks, we will do them an important service. Taking time at the beginning of the course to show them how the book works will pay off later on.

Teaching Students to Use a Handbook as a Writing Guide

Much of the advice given in the preceding section anticipates what I want to say here. Demystifying your handbook, teaching students how it works, is the necessary condition for using it effectively as a writing guide. Simply telling your students that they *should* consult the book is not likely to get results. And even after you have given them a thorough introductory tour of the text, students are apt to leave the book on the shelf unless you make an ongoing effort to see that they don't.

To assign the book as a writing guide means, in effect, to give it a prominent place in your course, even though you might not teach from it regularly. Other texts, perhaps a collection of readings or your students' own writing, may occupy most of the available class time. Students may spend a typical class period discussing a reading from an anthology, analyzing a sample paper, or working in groups on their drafts. While you may assign readings from the handbook to the entire class, you will not generally spend time going over the readings. The book thus becomes a resource that students use, mainly outside of class, to locate advice about writing, revising, and editing their work. Especially in classes organized as workshops, with the emphasis on practice and peer review, taking time to teach directly from the book, to use it as a classroom text, can disrupt the core activities of the course. Still, most instructors who conduct their classes in this fashion feel the need for an anchor text, a book that students can study and consult as needed for authoritative advice about writing. The handbook can fill this need. But without "teaching" the book, how can you ensure that your students will actually benefit from its advice?

Following are some suggestions for integrating your handbook into a course without making it the primary teaching text. Although these strategies require little class time, they should promote students' active use of the book as a writing guide and reference tool.

1. **Make the handbook a presence in the classroom**. Bring the book to class, even when you don't plan to teach from it, and encourage students to do likewise. By keeping the book in a handy spot on your desk—perhaps alongside a dictionary—you can easily consult it when needed during class discussions, demonstrating in a tangible way its value as a writing guide and *showing* students how to use the book to answer questions. If, for example, a student asks you during an editing session, "Should I use a semicolon or a colon here?" turn to the book with the student and look up the answer. Doing so will take a bit more time, of course, than simply saying which mark is appropriate, but looking up the information will *show* the student how to use the book for reference. And the next time an editing question comes up, the student may turn to the handbook before asking you.

   You can also spend a few minutes with the book at the beginning of each class as a way to start the conversation. For example, you might ask a student to read aloud one of the vignettes about language in everyday use that open most chapters. Discussing a vignette can help link the handbook's advice to the world outside the classroom. Alternatively, you can draw attention to some other spot in the book—one of the many shaded guideline boxes or a fine point of usage that you want students to review. Any of these activities should take no more than five minutes, but if one of them leads to a longer discussion about writing, so much the better.

2. **Ensure that reading assignments from the handbook reinforce other activities in the course**. Even if you don't "teach" the handbook, you can ask your students to read particular sections that directly support the work they are doing at the time. This may seem like an obvious point, yet I have seen many syllabi over the years that take precisely the opposite tack, having students read about sentence grammar while writing first drafts. Though there may be a certain logic in reviewing "basics" in the early part of a course, it is nearly always preferable, I think, to make as close a match as possible between handbook readings and the actual writing tasks that students are working on at the time. If, for example, you plan to have students bring draft thesis statements and outlines to class for discussion, you might ask them to read the sections on exploring, planning, and drafting in advance. You may not discuss them explicitly, but the students' reading will be directly relevant to the planned activity.

The goal is to make as close a match as possible between the book's advice and what you want your students to accomplish. The first time students revise a paper, they should be reading sections on reviewing, revising, and editing. Later, when they are revising, say, the third paper of the term, you might want them to pay close attention to sentence style. During that week of revision, then, you could assign one or more of the chapters on sentence style. For instance, you might ask students to study one of the chapters on sentence style and apply one or two of its lessons in reshaping their drafts. Or, if you want students to pay special attention to the use of commas during the final edit of a paper, you could assign the chapter on commas just prior to the edit. At that juncture, students will have a more pressing need for advice about commas (your pointed insistence that they get them right) than they will later. Again, the closer link you can make between the handbook and the students' writing projects, the more likely they are to use the book and to become comfortable with it as a guide to writing.

Other sorts of links are possible, too. If you plan to use a reader with the handbook, you may spend a good deal of class time discussing selections from the reader. The handbook can be a useful adjunct. For example, the critical reading or thinking chapters might serve over the term as a way to help students approach all their assignments from the reader. Likewise, if you plan to teach students to read argumentative essays or newspaper editorials, you might ask them to review, for example, the chapter on analyzing arguments. Or, if you are using the book in a literature-based course, sections on writing in the humanities will help students make reading-writing connections. Finally, at various points in the term, you may want to link the handbook's advice on creating online texts with work your students are doing online.

3. **Teach students to use the Top Twenty and early sections as a mini-handbook**. In addition to using "The Top Twenty: A Quick Guide to Troubleshooting Your Writing" and "Expectations for College Writing" (or "Find It. Fix It" and "A Writer's Choices" in *EasyWriter*) to orient students to the book, these sections have another potential use; together, they can serve throughout the term as a "mini-handbook," a freestanding section that students can use as a point of first reference to answer many of their most pressing questions. You may find it worthwhile, then, to spend time during the first week of class discussing the principles set forth in these sections and teaching students how to use these pages for reference.

You can begin by explaining that the Top Twenty is based on research conducted by Andrea Lunsford in 2006 and that its discussion of what constitutes good writing is grounded in the actual responses of college teachers to student papers. You should explain, in particular, that the material about broad content issues, organization, and presentation gives a decidedly realistic picture of what readers expect. Students should study this material early in the course and, if necessary, review it each time they begin a new paper.

What makes this material especially helpful is its emphasis on making students *independent*, its insistence that they take responsibility for their own writing. Students are advised to step back and look critically at their work—at details of expression as well as at larger issues of purpose, organization, and supporting evidence. The handbook shows them that good writing is always based on rhetorical choices made by responsible, well-informed writers.

The book's emphasis on responsibility is nowhere more apparent than in the discussion of surface errors. Here Lunsford urges students to take charge of their writing by charting their errors and learning to edit independently. As with the advice about content and organization, the treatment of surface errors is research-based, identifying the twenty most common errors actually marked in student papers and showing several examples of each error. Examples are shown hand-edited, so that students can see the error and its correction at a glance.

If the book as a whole can overwhelm some students with its comprehensive coverage of grammar, punctuation, and mechanics, the introduction should help sort things out. The information found in this part of the book is focused and to the point. Students can use it quickly at the beginning of the course to identify the errors most apt to appear in their work. Later, when they get back their marked drafts and finished papers, they can turn to the Top Twenty for quick reference. What they find there may be all they need. But if they want more advice, cross-references will send them to the relevant parts of the book. In marking papers, you might even want to do what one of my colleagues does: note errors in the margins with numbers (1 through 20), referring students directly to the condensed information in the introduction. If students learn to use that information intelligently, they are well on their way to becoming competent editors and proofreaders of their own work.

4. **Encourage students to use the handbook during peer-review sessions**. Many writing teachers make collaboration a regular part of their courses. For each paper, students spend time in small groups, responding to classmates' drafts and revising their work in light of the commentary they receive. These peer-review sessions provide good opportunities for students to use the handbook as a reference guide. You can even require that they do so.

Tell students in advance the specific issues you will ask them to consider when reading drafts, and ask them to study—before coming to class—the sections of the book relevant to those issues. With the first paper of the term, for example, a peer-review session might focus on issues of thesis and organization. Having reviewed these sections of the book beforehand, students will be prepared to use a shared vocabulary and set of assumptions in discussing one another's work. The handbook thus becomes a point of reference as well as a tool they can use to teach one another. Instead of saying (or writing on a peer-review sheet), "Your thesis is kind of vague," a student might say, "Your thesis states a topic, but it doesn't make a comment on the topic," or "Your thesis contains a workable comment, but is the idea really manageable for a four-page paper?" Your handbook's section on peer review offers specific advice, including guidelines on responding to drafts and the tools available to aid in peer review. Students can refer to the text to make their points, showing one another where to find additional advice. Thus, the book can give students the terms—and the terminology—they need to become effective peer reviewers. With practice, even inexperienced writers can develop considerable facility in helping their peers, and themselves, to use the book skillfully.

The same principles apply, of course, to students working independently outside of class: the more skillful they become at using the handbook, the more likely they are to keep it open on their desks as they revise. To encourage them, you might even ask that they turn in a brief response with a draft, or with the final copy of a paper, telling you two or three specific questions that they were able to resolve with help from the book.

5. **Use the handbook when marking drafts and grading finished papers**. When new instructors ask me whether they should use revision symbols, such as those found at the back of the handbook, when marking papers, I equivocate. On the one hand, the symbols are a convenient form of shorthand that can save a good deal of "grading time." On the other hand, if overused, the symbols can overwhelm students, who are more apt in theory than in practice to look up the indicated pages and read the information they find there. My advice usually comes down to this: use a few key symbols to identify common surface errors, but concentrate on larger issues (thesis, development, structure) and on persistent *patterns* of error that need attention. How is the handbook best used for this sort of marking?

Perhaps the best strategy is to mark selectively and to tie marginal and terminal comments as closely as possible to advice in the book. If, for example, a central weakness of a draft happens to be paragraph coherence, you might describe the problem in a sentence or two. Your comment, like a revision symbol, can send the student to the handbook, but whereas the symbol (*coh*) gives the student an entire section to read, your advice can be more specific: "Revise this paragraph by adding transitions between the sentences I've marked. See page xxx in the handbook." Supplying this degree of specificity takes time, but if marking is selective, if you focus on one or two major issues per paper, students are more likely to revise—and to use the book as a reference tool—than they are if you mark every error. Your terminal comment can help focus a student's attention, highlighting strengths to exploit and problems to avoid in the next draft. You might also point students to the chart of instructor comments in the handbook, which aids students in understanding frequently made comments by instructors.

The handbook can also be used in a like manner to mark surface errors. If you notice a persistent error in a student's writing—say, sentence fragments—you can repair two or three examples of the error (rather than marking all of them) and write a marginal comment to give advice. Again, this is the sort of advice that students can apply during revision, using your comments in tandem with a specific section of the book. The more selective and pointed you can make your comments, even if this means making fewer of them, the more your students will be inclined to act on the advice you give them—and to develop the habit of using the handbook for reference when working on their own.

Encouraging Students to Use the Handbook beyond First-Year Composition

Just as you may have started your first-year composition course by orienting students to the book, you may want to end it by explaining how the text can serve them in their other college courses. You might even choose to devote part of a class period to another guided tour of the book, highlighting sections that students will find most helpful in subsequent courses.

You can begin the tour by letting students know that the kind of writing they have been doing in your class has much in common with the writing they will be asked to do later. For that reason, they may want to revisit the chapters on the writing process often; their research-based overview of the qualities of good academic writing, their emphasis on rhetorical effectiveness, and their attention to reader expectations apply to written communication in all disciplines. The Top Twenty also serves as a quick reference on common errors, and and the chapters on writing in the disciplines are bound to be helpful. It is also worth reminding students of the enormous amount of all-purpose information in the handbook—advice about the writing process, chapters on surface errors and punctuation, chapters on word choice, and much more.

Reminding your students of the various ways they might use the handbook beyond first-year composition helps place the courses you teach in a larger academic context. Students at the outset of their college years rarely see the "big picture"; they often have little sense of the interconnectedness of the curriculum they are beginning to pursue. You should do what you can to show them the connections—especially the way in which writing, as a way of learning and as a means of communication, cuts across disciplinary boundaries. In a small but significant way, teaching students to make the handbook a trusted guide and reference companion contributes to that effort.

The Top Twenty: A Quick Guide to Troubleshooting Your Writing

Overview

Recent research on students' approaches to college-level writing indicates that students are deeply invested in improving their rhetorical and argumentative skills in a way that confirms our scholarly insistence on "process" methodologies. As Richard Light discovered through his interviews with Harvard undergraduates, students not only are open to working through the acts of invention, organization, revision, and editing but in fact desire the opportunity to do so. In his study entitled *Making the Most of College: Students Speak Their Minds*, Light reflects:

> The findings from our survey dramatize the extraordinary importance that students put on good writing. . . . I was surprised by students' strong attitude toward writing. I would have guessed that they value good writing, but I didn't realize how deeply many of them care about it, or how strongly they hunger for specific suggestions about how to improve it.

Similarly, students at Stanford University told a group of writing teachers that they desired the freedom to make mistakes in their writing and rhetoric classes. They also voiced a hunger to take risks, receive suggestions, and analyze texts that they might use as models.

Our challenge as teachers is to provide the space for such risk-taking to occur. We might reconceptualize writing as an inevitable process of working through errors. In the words of Malcolm Gladwell, journalist for the *New Yorker* and author of *The Tipping Point*, the writer's inclination is to err. "Journalists write a lot," Gladwell told an audience at Stanford University in January 2002, "so sometimes you are just wrong."

Allowing—even encouraging—our students to embrace experimentation and error as integral parts of the writing process empowers them as practitioners and rhetoricians; it also provides us as teachers the opportunity to take risks in our facilitation of writing exercises and assignments. Above all, our task is to foster *critical thinking* about the errors—and the exceptional rhetorical strategies—in all writing. In this way, we can invite students to develop the ability to analyze the rhetorical situations in the textual, visual, and multimedia world around them and to transform their engagement into effective writing that contributes to the public sphere.

The Top Twenty encourages students to begin taking risks—not to fear failure, but to seize the opportunity to shape language into elegant, persuasive texts of rhetorical power and significance.

Teaching Advice: Taking a Writing Inventory

One way to encourage students to begin actively learning from their errors is through the use of writing inventories. Writing inventories help students take stock of their writing and think critically and analytically about how to improve their writing skills. After students have completed their first few assignments and have had time to review your comments, ask them to take a writing inventory using these ten steps:

1. Assemble copies of your first two or three pieces of writing, making sure to select those to which either your instructor or other students have responded.

2. Read through this writing, adding your own comments about its strengths and weaknesses.

3. Examine the instructor and peer comments carefully, and compare them with your own comments.

4. Group all the comments into the categories discussed in the Top Twenty.

5. Make an inventory of your own strengths in each category.

6. Study your errors, marking every instructor and peer comment that suggests or calls for an improvement and putting them all in a list.

7. Consult the appropriate sections of your book for more detailed help in those areas where you need it.

8. Make up a priority list of three or four particular writing problems you have identified, and write out a plan for improvement.

9. Note at least two strengths you want to build on in your writing.

10. Record your findings in a writing log, which you can add to as the class proceeds.

Before you ask students to take a full inventory of their writing, you might consider working through the beginning of a hypothetical inventory with them. To do so, distribute copies of a student essay (from your files or from another class), and ask the students to work with you to identify broad content issues, strengths or weaknesses in organization and language, and surface or citation errors.

To give students practice in taking a writing inventory on a more detailed level, ask them to examine a piece of writing for some specific feature—looking for every organizational "cue," for instance, or every transitional word or phrase. They can do this part of the assignment particularly well in groups. Then ask them to reflect on their findings and to draw one or more conclusions. Such an exercise asks students to move from observation to generalization, to "metadiscourse" about their own writing, or to what Shirley Brice Heath calls building theories about their own language use. The more students are able to make such mental moves, the better they will be at monitoring their own learning and at learning from their own errors.

Teaching Advice: Looking for Strengths in Student Writing

Peter Elbow reminds us that it is characteristic of good teachers to *like* student writing, even though they see its weaknesses or failures. Elbow urges teachers to cultivate their enjoyment of student writing by (1) looking for "strengths, both real and potential"; (2) practicing "conscious, disciplined, positive reinforcement"; and (3) getting to know students through conferences, journals, and free topic choices. Elbow concludes: "It's not improving our writing that leads us to like it, but rather our liking it that leads us to improving it. Liking writing makes it easier to criticize it—and makes criticism easier to take and to learn from." (Lecture delivered at Bread Loaf School of English, July 17, 1991)

Teaching Advice: Learning from Your Errors

The greater the writer's fixation on error, the greater the difficulty that writer will have writing. The more the instructor focuses on error, the more the student will worry about error. In *The Concept of the Mind*, British philosopher Gilbert Ryle wrote that "errors are exercises in competence." And this new concept of error as "portals to discovery" became the mainstay of Mina Shaughnessy's study of basic writing. By 1981, Isabella Halsted was writing that errors are "*not* Sin, not Crime punishable by F." Errors are simply mistakes that we are all capable of, given the wrong circumstances: lack of sleep, deadline pressure, unfamiliarity with formal English. In "Putting Error in Its Place," Halsted describes her own attitude toward error:

> Like soot on the pane, Error is something that gets in the way of the clear vision. . . . Error on all levels is distracting, annoying, obstructive. Error is inexcusable ultimately, yes, [but] not because it is Wrong per se. . . . In plain pragmatic terms, the absence of Error is useful; but when our students take pains to avoid it—by writing short sentences, by sticking to one tense, by writing as little as possible—I doubt very much that they do so in order to better communicate with a reader, but rather to play safe, to avoid the red marks.

At the same time, however, research by Larry Beason, in "Ethos and Error," suggests that errors impede more than communication; they also endanger a writer's credibility and character. Through quantitative research on fourteen businesspeople, Beason offers a rhetorical analysis of errors in terms of how textual transgressions lead readers to produce judgments of character and consequently construct "a negative ethos of the writer."

Beason's study provides compelling reasons for teachers to spend time helping students identify common errors in their writing: "Whether we believe it to be the optimum situation or not, errors have an impact on the writer's image and communicability. Error avoidance, I submit, should have a presence in the composition curriculum—but without overpowering it." Focusing students' attention on the "Top Twenty" can go a long way toward remedying such ethos-damaging errors.

Teaching Advice: The Top Twenty

Here are twenty passages taken from the group of student essays on which Lunsford and Lunsford's research is based. Each passage contains one of the twenty most common student writing errors, and these passages are numbered to correspond with the Top Twenty list in the handbook. These passages may be used in at least three different ways: (1) you might reproduce this list and use it as a diagnostic test early in the semester to see how practiced your students are at recognizing these errors; (2) you might use the passages as a review test at the end of the semester or after concluding your class's study of this introduction; (3) you may simply want to use them as examples of the Top Twenty errors, supplementing those given in the text. After giving students this list, you can also use the following assignment in class.

1. These essays were very contrasting.

2. The Beast which is one of the biggest roller coasters, has a thunderous ride of steep hills and turns. As you race down the first and biggest hill your coaster is engulfed by a tunnel at the end of the hill.

3. The author insists that the fur trade "is a game for wise old wolves, not new tenderfeet and fly-by-night gamblers."

4. Once you find where other surfers are, you can set up your camp. This entails claiming your own territory. You do this by laying out your oversized beach towel and by turning your radio on loud enough to mark your domain without disturbing anyone else. This should help you blend in with the locals.

5. Can we not say that statistics bare witness?

6. In "The Last Drop", he tries to explain why so many parts of the world do not have a regular supply of clean water.

7. There is also a stand up roller coaster called, the King Kobra, which goes upside down in the first loop, with plenty of tossing and turning. Like I said previously, King's Island also keeps the people with weaker stomachs in mind; there are rides all throughout the park which are a little slower paced.

8. The choices for English Language Learners are limited; Either assimilate quickly or be segregated.

9. After deciding to begin their college careers, many students are faced with the predicament of where to live. This is not such a problem for students from out of town, but it is for those who live in the same area which they attend school.

10. To give a recent example, Ellen Barry reported on a judge in Lebanon, Tennessee, who was presiding over a hearing of a child abuse case in which the person being charged was an eighteen-year-old immigrant mother, ordered to not only learn English but to learn it at the fourth grade proficiency by the next hearing.

11. The knights with armor and horses beautifully decorated participate in battles of jousting, target shooting with spears, archery, and duels of strategy and strength using swords and shields. During the evening, there is a break from the fighting, and a beautiful ceremony of marriage is acted out.

12. The good thing about its location is that it is right off the main highway, very easy to spot. There are also plenty of road signs pointing you in the direction of the park. And if you got extremely lost, pulling off and asking would be the easiest way to get on track.

13. I was gaining speed and feeling really good but when I looked back he wasn't there. I panicked. I saw him and my parents down at the other end of the street and forgot to look forward. When I finally did turn forward, I saw that I was rapidly closing in on my neighbor's car. How ironic; I was about to hit the car of the man who was trying to teach me how to ride a bike.

14. What I'm trying to get at is that because of this persons immaturity, many people have suffered. This persons lack of responsibility has turned peoples lives upside down.

15. I felt someone's hand shaking my shoulder. I lifted my head up to see my best friend Stephanie looking down at me. "That must have been some dream. Come on the bell rang class is over."

16. Chips and sauces are not the only thing that you get free refills on, you also get free refills on all non-alcoholic beverages, such as soda and tea. The servers are very good about getting you more of both things when you need refills, usually you do not even have to ask.

17. On the other hand, what if you don't care for your partner—or even worse—they don't care for you? You know now that it is still okay to separate without the problem of obtaining a divorce. Many divorces that take place within the first years of marriage might have been avoided if the couple had lived together before marrying.

18. According to the *New York Times*, an open government site published "The documents, the experts say, constitute a basic guide to building an atom bomb" (Broad A1).

19. Her free-spirit was obvious in her artwork.

20. When I got to half court, the guy that was playing center on my team stood between the defensive player and me. As I dribbled around the center, he stopped the defensive player. Not by using his hands but by his big body. This is a strategy used to get a player open for a shot.

Activity: The Top Twenty

Ask students to work in groups of three to compare findings and plans for improvement after working through the previous twenty passages. Their first plan should be to categorize the errors they make according to the catalog of errors in this chapter. Then they may want to determine the frequency of errors they make in each category. This simple exercise will establish their ability to evaluate their own work, an important skill each writer needs to develop.

Rhetorical Situations

Overview

No writing takes place in isolation. As Wayne C. Booth wrote in his classic essay "The Rhetorical Stance," all good writing establishes a relationship among content, reader, and writer. In texts from emails to research papers, there is a dynamic interplay among audience, persona, and message that signifies the "rhetorical situation." As they embark on a writing endeavor, your students will engage with this dynamic.

Teaching Advice: Understanding Rhetorical Situations

You can provide students with experience writing in a variety of academic genres by offering them freedom to choose the rhetorical stance for a particular assignment. Have them select the disciplinary parameters for their essays by modeling their work on published academic writing in the fields of literary analysis, film review, scientific writing, social science research, or computer science. A good way to develop students' critical reading and writing skills in terms of genre and academic discourse is to ask them to find a contemporary article on a subject of their choice from a recent periodical or academic journal. Conduct a rhetorical analysis of the article, examining the genre for its specific writing conventions. Then have students model their own writing after the article's discipline-specific attributes.

Teaching Advice: Understanding Academic Assignments

Some instructors—and writing programs—believe that three to five pages is an appropriate page length for most composition-course essays. Three- to five-page papers demand development of a topic beyond simple description of a problem or narration of an event, yet they are short enough to require significant narrowing of the topic. In contrast, other instructors require progressively longer and more challenging assignments, culminating in a fifteen- to twenty-page research paper. Whatever the length of the assignment, take the time to create *detailed* and *directive* assignment sheets that explain the purpose, goals, length, format, content, and grading criteria for the assignment. It is often helpful to break down these items into categories and to offer models to help students begin the writing project.

Consider assigning due dates for drafts. A day or two after introducing invention strategies, assign an exploratory draft. A couple of days later, schedule conferences with your students to discuss their work. Within the next few days, have them bring their revisions—along with all their planning notes and earlier drafts—to class. Setting deadlines for drafts reinforces the importance of starting early.

After designing and distributing your assignment, make time in class to read through the detailed handout and answer any questions. Too often we leave this step up to the students and, consequently, problems arise concerning expectations, which could have been avoided with a general class discussion. Stress the importance of comprehending and addressing the rhetorical situation before beginning to write.

Choices about Topics

Ask your students to keep a section in their writing logs dedicated to compiling essay topics on subjects that interest them. The log can also be a place to store ideas, intriguing facts, observations, and provocative quotations from public figures or from students' reading (academic or otherwise). Organizing these entries under general subject headings (of the teacher's suggestion or the writer's invention) can provide some initial development of the topics.

Rhetorical Stance

The idea of the rhetorical stance was first put forward by Wayne Booth in a *CCC* article of the same name. A good rhetorical stance, said Booth, was the result of an effective balance among the three Aristotelian forms of proof: *ethos, pathos,* and *logos.* Too much emphasis on *ethos,* the wonderfulness of the writer, would result in an imbalance that Booth called the entertainer's stance. Too much emphasis on *pathos,* playing to the desires of the audience, would result in the advertiser's stance. And too much emphasis on *logos,* the message in itself, would result in the imbalance that Booth called the pedant's stance. Keeping these three elements at work but not allowing any one to predominate is the work of the successful writer.

Activity: Thinking about Topics

Use small groups to generate ten to twenty possible topics or questions for several subject areas, such as interesting people, current controversies, cultural trends, problems on campus, scientific discoveries we'd like to know more about, possibilities for progress or decay, and so on. Students can use these topics or questions as starters for prewriting activities, which may lead directly to an essay draft.

Activity: Purposes for Academic Writing

Ask students to join with two other members of the class. Each team should choose one of the following assignments and describe its various purposes. Have students take notes during their collaborative work and bring their notes to class for discussion.

1. Compare two book-length studies of Malcolm X.
2. Discuss the controversies surrounding the use of genetic engineering to change characteristics of unborn children.

3. Analyze the use of headlines in a group of twenty advertisements.

4. Describe a favorite spot in your hometown.

5. Explain the concept of virtual reality.

Teaching Advice: Prewriting

Whether the stimulus for writing comes from outside the writer (as in a class assignment) or grows from the writer's own desire to put thoughts into words, the decision to write is a deliberate act of commitment. When we commit ourselves to writing, we *prewrite* by assessing our writing (that is, rhetorical) situation, asking ourselves questions such as the following: Who is my audience? What does the audience expect of me? What do I already know about this subject? What must I find out? How can I best arrange my information and ideas? How much time do I have? How long should the composition be?

As soon as you make a writing assignment, encourage your students to respond to these questions by "thinking with a pencil in hand," jotting down ideas in their writing logs. Unlike experienced writers, students tend to spend little time prewriting. You might want to remind your students that almost all writers, even experienced ones, dread the blank page. Many authors say that the quickest way to face that challenge is to cover the blank page with writing, allowing anything to find its way onto the page.

Teaching Advice: Considering Audiences

In *A Pedagogy of Possibility*, Kay Halasek discusses audience in ways that are helpful to teachers and students alike. Halasek briefly describes the uses of six kinds of audience that writers have available to them: projected audience (those imagined or invoked by the writer), previous audience (those the writer is responding to or is in conversation with), immediate audience (such as peer group members), textual audience (what some call the "implied" reader or the audience in the text), public audience (those to whom the text will be sent), and evaluative audience (the teacher, employer, or group that will assess the text).

Dealing with questions of audience is one of the most complex problems facing any writer, and face-to-face oral communication doesn't completely prepare students for the intricacies of attending to audience in written texts. Discuss the six types of audience presented above with your students and ask them to brainstorm examples of each type from their daily lives. Try the exercises that follow to continue educating students about the crucial importance of audience in the writing process.

Ask students to prepare to write an essay describing the college health service's policies on distribution of birth control information. They should answer the questions analyzing audiences listed in this section for two audiences: a women's student group at another college and a religious-based scholarship committee. This exercise can be done either individually or in groups, and in either case the writing is followed by class discussion on the kinds of problems each audience presents to a writer.

A student's first response to the question of audience is usually to assume that the instructor is the audience as well as the evaluator of the essay. Help your students distinguish between the two by asking them to write a *general audience profile*. If, for example, their general topic is *part-time worker, full-time student*, their audience profile might read something like this: *My audience is seventeen- and eighteen-year-olds who are either attending or planning to attend college and who have experienced the dual obligations of work and school.*

By writing an audience profile for each paper, your students will begin to see that they are constructing an audience that goes beyond you. As they begin to visualize their audience, they can write directly to it instead of directly for you. It will also be easier for you to evaluate their work when they have defined their audience.

You many want to follow this up with one of the following activities on audiences.

Activity: Audiences for Formal and Academic Writing

Ask each student to bring in an article, editorial, or column from the newspaper and to circle elements in the writing that deliberately include or exclude certain kinds of audiences. Ask students to read the circled excerpts and talk about whether the writer seemed to be aware of or in control of his or her effects, and how and why the writer made the choices he or she made concerning the inclusion or exclusion of audiences. Ask students to bring in local newspapers and magazines that target speakers of languages other than English. Discuss the audiences for each periodical.

Activity: Specific Audiences and Peer Response

If your students are working on an essay, have them exchange their drafts and write audience profiles based on one another's topics. After they have returned the profiles and drafts, the students may need to rethink their original audience. This type of collaborative work often helps students grasp the significance of addressing an audience and the way in which they need to revise their stance, strategic use of appeals, and language to match readers' expectations.

Teaching Advice: Analyze Your Position as a Writer or Speaker

Students may have trouble coming up with a succinct statement of purpose for a piece of writing they are currently working on. Often their purpose will be little more than a simple statement like *My purpose is to tell the story of how I felt after I wrecked my dad's Buick* or *My purpose is to describe how stupid it is to shoplift.* Try pushing students beyond these simple statements into purpose statements that include some effect on the audience, since audience and purpose are always linked. The intended audience for most first drafts is usually either *people in the class*, or *you, the instructor*. Again, asking students to go beyond audiences that are immediately available will increase their repertoire of abilities. In talking with or writing to the student, keep asking how the writing would change if written for some other audience.

Activity: Analyze Your Position as a Writer or Speaker

Ask students to join with two other members of the class and reconsider one of the assignments from the "Purposes for Academic Writing" activity on page 64, this time focusing on their positions as writers or speakers. Have students take notes during their collaborative work and bring their notes to class for discussion.

1. Compare two book-length studies of Malcolm X.

2. Discuss the controversies surrounding the use of genetic engineering to change characteristics of unborn children.

3. Analyze the use of headlines in a group of twenty advertisements, and then analyze what relationship those headlines have to the visual image in the advertisement.

4. Describe a favorite spot in your hometown.

5. Explain the concept of virtual reality.

Activity: Tone and Style 1

To help students consider how words and images work together to create tone, ask them to gather a collection of magazine advertisements. As a class, analyze a few ads, closely reading and assessing how the text works—or doesn't work—with the visuals in the ads. Engage in a large-group discussion about the arguments that advertisements make to us, as potential consumers, through text and through images. Then explore possible examples of resistance or appropriation—for instance, the "spoof ads" hosted at adbusters.org (adbusters.org/spoofads). Finally, ask students to choose a particular ad and to revise or rewrite the text. For instance, the text for an ad for couture jeans that features a thin model might read "Skip lunch, buy our jeans." An ad for beer that features a fit man with exposed and muscled abdominals might read "Beer gut?" An ad for deodorant that promises a "radical breakthrough in dryness protection" might be revised to read "Once upon a time in America, revolution meant the overthrow of a government and radical meant never-before-known ideas and discoveries."

Activity: Tone and Style 2

In addition or as an alternative to the preceding exercise, ask students working in pairs or small groups to visit the Web sites of different types of organizations or businesses (for example, museums, nonprofits, hospitals). Have each group identify the type of site they are exploring and present to the class how visuals are used within the site to create a feel, a voice, an identity, and a tone. Then ask students to find and carefully read the mission statement or "About Us" sections of the sites and analyze how effectively the tone of the writing matches the tone of the imagery.

Resources

Section	The St. Martin's Handbook	The Everyday Writer	EasyWriter
Understanding Rhetorical Situations	2–2a	5b	1
Understanding Academic Assignments	2b	5b	1a–1b
Choices about Topics	2c1	5c	1c
Rhetorical Stance	2c2	5e	1e
Purposes for Academic Writing	2c3	5d	1b
Considering Audiences	2d	5c	1d
Tone and Style	2f	5f	1e

Note: Depending on which book you are using, student essays may appear online rather than in print. Check the Directory of Student Writing for locations.

Thesis

Overview

Classical rhetoric consisted of five canons: *inventio* (invention), *dispositio* (arrangement), *elocutio* (style), *memoria* (memory), and *pronunciatio* (delivery). The process of discovery implied by the Latin *inventio* and the Greek *heuresis* parallels our modern concept of prewriting. Since *prewriting* is often used to refer both to "invention" and to "planning," your students might want to think of invention as a process of exploring what to say about a topic; of planning as the choices of what, when, and how to say it; and of prewriting as the first stage in the writing process, when invention and planning most often occur. While drafting can and should occur throughout exploring and planning, at some point you will want to help students compile all their drafting into an official first draft. Encourage your students to be creative in their approach to a topic, the prewriting process, and the planning of organizational strategies.

Teaching Advice: Exploring a Topic

Exploring a topic through brainstorming works particularly well with groups of three to five students, but it generates even more energy when conducted with the entire class. Whether you or your students suggest the topic is not as important as getting started.

Appoint two students to record ideas as they are suggested by the rest of the class. After about ten minutes, break the class into groups of four and ask each group to choose an idea and develop a thesis from it. Share with your students the following ways to facilitate brainstorming:

- Write down as many ideas as you can think of *without stopping*. Go back and edit your list later, selecting the most promising topics.

- Speak into a voice recorder as you walk through campus, commenting on what you notice as interesting.

- Keep a reaction journal in which you jot down your responses to course lectures, reading materials, news items, and public conversations in dining halls or on the street.

- Find the most provocative article you can on a topic that matters to you, and forge a constructive response to it.

- Interview five people in your community on a matter of historical, intellectual, or personal interest. Transcribe their responses into a dialogue, and insert your own voice in an attempt to discover your own stance.

Brainstorming

Peter Elbow suggests in *Writing without Teachers* that students who sincerely want to improve their writing keep a freewriting diary. This is a great way to work on brainstorming topics. He writes:

> Just ten minutes a day. Not a complete account of your day; just a brief mind sample for each day. You don't have to think hard or prepare or be in the mood: without stopping, just write whatever words come out—whether or not you are thinking or in the mood.

Freewriting and Looping

James Moffett, in *Teaching the Universe of Discourse*, and Janet Emig, in *The Composing Processes of Twelfth Graders*, posit that freewriting not only increases verbal fluency but also provides a means for discovering ideas. In *Writing without Teachers*, Peter Elbow writes:

> The habit of compulsive, premature editing doesn't just make writing hard. It makes writing dead. Your voice is damped out by all the interruptions, changes, and hesitations between the consciousness and the page.

Freewriting eliminates the beginning writer's most frustrating habit: focusing on correctness rather than content. During final drafting, your students will need to focus on correctness—but not until then.

Looping is a way to activate students' critical thinking. If you are teaching with a course email distribution list or a bulletin board, have each student post an initial one- to two-sentence description of an idea that might provide the beginning of a paper. Then ask students to respond to one or two posts and identify what is most interesting about the topics. Have the first student, in turn, respond to the reactions of the class by developing and amplifying the focus of the topic. This form of collaborative looping, facilitated by technology, can offer a fast and meaningful way to encourage your students' exploration of writing topics.

Clustering

The software program Inspiration enables students to follow the flow of their ideas through diagrams that resemble clouds, circles, or squares. Arrows can begin to show relations between items and, with the click of a drop-down menu, students can convert their clusters of ideas into an outline.

Activity: Drafting a Working Thesis

Have students exchange their working theses and peer evaluation, using questions such as these:

1. Does the thesis arouse your interest? How can it be made more engaging?
2. Is the thesis clear and specific? How can the writer make it more so?

3. What is the "so what?" of the thesis? How might the writer push the argument further?

4. Does the thesis seem manageable within the limits of time and length? Does the writer promise to do too much? How can the writer narrow the thesis?

The value of this peer-review exercise is greater perspective. What is patently obvious to the writer may not be so discernible to a reader whose information is limited to the text.

Teaching Advice: Gathering Information

Many students—including juniors and seniors—have little experience with research projects or familiarity with the campus library. You might consider holding a class in the library and arranging for a reference librarian to describe the general resources of the library (including electronic resources) and to explain their location and usefulness.

Activity: Gathering Information

There are a variety of ways to orient students to the wealth of materials available to them in the form of verbal and visual information for writing projects. Your own field research into the ever-increasing information available to students will help make their research projects more exciting.

- Explore the online resources of your institution's library and research facilities in order to point students to helpful resources.
- Look into archives and special collections that host specialized information in terms of documents, visual material, digitized collections, sound collections, and more.
- Investigate your institution's office of undergraduate research to find out if there are Web sites listing faculty mentors (for possible interviews), scholarships and research grant opportunities for students (for continuation of their projects), and workshops in research skills on campus.

Activity: Organizing Verbal and Visual Information 1

Ask students to decide which method (or methods) of organization they would recommend to students writing on the following topics, and why. This activity will give students practice before they turn to their own writing projects.

1. the need for a new undergraduate library
2. the autobiographical elements in Virginia Woolf's *To the Lighthouse*
3. why voting rates in U.S. elections are low
4. the role of education in preventing the spread of AIDS
5. the best contemporary rap artist or group

Activity: Organizing Verbal and Visual Information 2

For verbal composition, ask your students to read and comment on one another's drafts, looking first at organizational patterns in individual paragraphs and then throughout the entire paper. Ask them to write in the margin the type of paragraph organization. Toward the end of class, call on several students to read paragraphs that illustrate different forms of organization. Some paragraphs may defy classification because of the ingenuity of the writer or the rough condition of the draft.

Another effective teaching strategy entails asking students to produce an outline *after* completing their draft essays. Use these outlines to double-check the organization and flow of the essay as well as the strategic use of both visual and verbal information.

Teaching Advice: Planning

Even the most proficient predraft outliners need to know that outlines are not unalterable or absolute; they are merely guides. The outline must conform to the paper—not the paper to the outline. Outlines, like the papers they help organize, must be revisable.

If you require an unchangeable, formal outline, your students may not be able to adhere to it. Instead, ask them to prepare a writing plan, a backbone for the body of the paper. Then allow them to develop their papers as much by their drafting processes, which reveal form, as by their plan. Another possibility is to have them write each idea on a note card so they can easily rearrange their ideas and experiment with various orders. They will also learn that some ideas are expendable.

Teaching Advice: Drafting

Remind students that first drafts are never perfect. Among the many other scholars and researchers who believe that first drafts are rarely directed toward an audience, Linda Flower lists the features of what she calls "writer-based prose." According to Flower, this stage of writing is

1. typically narrative or chronological in structure
2. usually filled with private terms that may not be meaningful to another reader
3. sometimes elliptical
4. filled with unclear referents and causal relations
5. frequently loaded with self-referents such as "I believe," "I feel," "in my opinion"

Flower views writer-based prose as a natural stage in the composing process, one that allows for discovery and growth and that should not be criticized because it is not yet "reader-based." Often, proficient writers can skip the stage of writer-based prose and move directly to reader-based prose. These writers seem to internalize their writer-based drafts, unlike many beginning writers.

Anne Lamott's famous advice to writers in "Shitty First Drafts" in *Bird by Bird: Some Instructions on Writing and Life* merits repeating to students embarking on producing a draft: "Now, practically even better news than that of short assignments is the idea of shitty first drafts. All good writers write them. This is how they end up with good second drafts and terrific third drafts" (21).

Help students overcome their own fears about first drafts by giving them permission to make errors, to explore intellectual content, to try strategies of argument, and to play with variations in their writing style and persona. Allow them to experiment with voice in a first draft, to be comfortable with not having all the answers, and to write for the sake of discovering meaning. The open, encouraging attitude of a teacher can go a long way toward getting that first draft down on paper.

Resources

Section	The St. Martin's Handbook	The Everyday Writer	EasyWriter
Exploring a Topic	3a	6a–6g	2a
Drafting a Working Thesis	3c	7b	2b
Gathering Information	3d	7c	2c
Organizing Verbal and Visual Information	3e	7d	2d
Planning	3f	7e	2d
Drafting	3g	7f	2d

Note: Depending on which book you are using, student essays may appear online rather than in print. Check the Directory of Student Writing for locations.

Paragraphs

Overview

A good paragraph is an elusive entity. It is easy to explain the basics—the group of sentences set off in a paragraph should all aim at developing one main idea—but difficult to demonstrate all the varied forms that good paragraphs can take, as well as to help students improve their abilities to write cohesive paragraphs. The following advice and activities focus on the various skills that are necessary for writing strong, unified paragraphs, and should help strengthen students' abilities to understand the structure of the paragraphs that they read and use this understanding to improve their own writing.

Teaching Advice: Creating Strong Paragraphs

Students often have problems with conventional academic paragraphing—with development and cohesion. And their problems are often diagnosed in various ways. For instance, George Goodin and Kyle Perkins argue that because students fail to subordinate effectively, their writing is replete with digressions and afterthoughts. Betty Bamberg argues that cohesion comes with the successful movement from "writer-based" to "reader-based" prose. Writer-based prose often consists of elliptical expressions, sentences that have meaning for the writer but that omit information necessary for the reader's understanding.

Successful prewriting—and the kind of analysis Halasek calls on both students and instructors to do—may be the best cure for both of these paragraphing "problems." By planning ahead what to say and how to say it, writers can better stay on course. Therefore, reaffirm the need for prewriting as you introduce paragraphing. Adequate prewriting will result in the more orderly text characteristic of academic paragraphs.

Activity: Creating Strong Paragraphs

Encourage your students to browse through their favorite nonacademic reading materials—newspapers, magazines, novels, nonfiction, Web sites, blogs—looking for effective long and short paragraphs. They should bring their samples to class, either copies to be distributed or one copy to read aloud. Have students work in groups of three or four to explain the paragraphing conventions of their chosen publications and authors.

In small groups, they'll need to answer the following questions:

1. What idea or topic does each paragraph develop?
2. What special effects do the paragraphs create, if any?
3. How do these effects move forward the main idea?

This exercise will serve to heighten students' awareness of paragraphing techniques—their own as well as those of their favorite authors. Remind students that all writers tend to imitate the styles of their favorite authors, consciously and unconsciously.

Teaching Advice: Writing Unified Paragraphs

The notion that one sentence in every paragraph should announce the main idea of that paragraph was derived from the fourth law of Alexander Bain's "seven laws" for creating paragraphs: "Indication of theme: The opening sentence, unless obviously preparatory, is expected to indicate the scope of the paragraph."

Although most compositionists agree with Bain that every paragraph should have a unifying theme or purpose, not all agree that it should be announced by a topic sentence. In his study of professional writers, Richard Braddock found that topic sentences are used far less than we have traditionally believed; his research calls into question the teaching of topic sentences. On the other hand, Frank D'Angelo argues that despite Braddock's findings, the use of topic sentences improves the readability of a paragraph.

The following two activities should be of use in helping students develop their abilities to write unified paragraphs.

Activity: Writing Unified Paragraphs 1

If your class uses a reader, have students turn to *any* essay in it and see whether they can find a topic sentence in each paragraph. (1) What is the placement of the topic sentence? (2) What are the key terms in that topic sentence? (3) How does the information in that paragraph relate to those key words?

Ask students to repeat this exercise using their own drafts. With students working in small groups of two or three, project each student's essay on a shared plasma screen. Change the font color of the topic sentence of each paragraph. At the end of the allotted time, ask students to select three paragraphs from their papers that show different strategies for positioning a topic sentence. Display the models for the entire class, and discuss the pros and cons of each approach. Allow students to speak about their selections and to describe how the placement functions as a persuasive act.

Activity: Writing Unified Paragraphs 2

One practical way to have students check whether each sentence relates to the main idea of the paragraph is through a collaborative highlighting exercise. Ask students to exchange papers in writing groups. Have each student go through one essay, highlighting the main idea of each paragraph and noting the relevance of each sentence in a given paragraph to the highlighted one. Then ask the groups to discuss their reviews together. Provide them with the following questions to help their analysis:

- Does each paragraph stand on its own as a unified whole? Are there too many new ideas in a given paragraph?
- Do the details of each paragraph fit together to support the topic sentence?

Encourage the peer-review groups to revise one paragraph from each essay collaboratively by relying on the strengths of each group member.

Teaching Advice: Developing Paragraphs

No such thing as a pure definition or division/classification or comparison/contrast essay exists outside of the classroom, and to teach or assign these techniques as discourse structures is to confuse means with ends. Discourses are, perhaps without exception, motivated by multiple aims. However, we can identify primary aims and primary organizing principles in order to construct essays using dynamic and reciprocal notions of function and form.

Determining Paragraph Length

Modern stylist William Zinsser advises nonfiction writers to keep their paragraphs short. Visually, such paragraphs are more inviting because they have more white space around them. But he does not mean that all paragraphs should be the same length. Paragraph length should vary with purpose: long paragraphs often introduce a character, a setting, or a situation, whereas short paragraphs add emphasis or move the reader through the text.

Ask your students to find a magazine article and a newspaper article that cover the same story. Which medium has more consistent paragraph length? Is one story more in-depth? Does one have longer, more developed paragraphs that continue to introduce new information? Can students account for the different styles and lengths of paragraphs?

Then, you can use the following two exercises to help your students work on developing their paragraphs.

Activity: Developing Paragraphs 1

Have students work in pairs to rewrite the following undeveloped paragraphs by adding concrete supporting details, examples, and reasons. The groups should bring their collaboratively revised paragraphs to class for discussion.

1. *The introduction to an essay tentatively titled "A Week on $12.80":* Nothing is more frustrating to a college student than being dead broke. Not having money for enough food or for the rent, much less for entertainment, is not much fun. And of course debts for tuition and books keep piling up. No, being broke is not to be recommended.

2. *The introduction to a humorous essay contrasting cats and dogs:*

Have you threatened your cat lately? If not, why not? Why not get a real pet—a dog? Dogs, after all, are better pets. Cats, on the other hand, are a menace to the environment.

Activity: Developing Paragraphs 2

As a way of introducing the idea of logical patterns of development, consider asking the class to answer the following series of questions on their computers or through a threaded email discussion:

1. What are your strengths and weaknesses as a writer?
2. Is your writing process linear or recursive?
3. How do you learn in this class: from writing? from taking notes? from reading and responding to your friends' work?
4. What are your reasons for taking this course?

Then, with students working in groups of three, have them use their answers to these questions to classify each other into different groups. Ask students to draft a chart presenting the results of their classifications and to discuss different strategies for dividing and classifying. Project the results on a shared overhead screen to enable further class discussion.

Teaching Advice: Making Paragraphs Coherent

The notion of relational unity within discrete units received an added boost when Alexander Bain helped transform the field of rhetoric by emphasizing contiguity and similarity as the key processes of association implicit in rhetorical acts. You can encourage your students to think through these terms in order to produce associational paragraphs in which the details fit together in contiguous or similar ways. By allowing students to experiment with different types of organization—spatial, chronological, logical, and associational—you can teach them to see the pattern of relationality in all writing.

Here is some more specific advice for teaching students how to write coherent paragraphs, followed by two activities.

Repetition for Coherent Paragraphs

Repetition of key words and phrases is an age-old technique for pulling together thematically related units; moreover, the rhythm of such verbal/visual echoing effectively holds the audience's attention. We are all familiar with various repetitive devices.

Single word

Vanity of vanities, saith the preacher, vanity of vanities; all is vanity.   —Ecclesiasticus 1:1

Syntactic structure

The thoughts are but overflowings of the mind, and the tongue is but a servant of the thought.
—Philip Sidney

Anaphora (initial repetition)

Say that I was a drum major for justice. Say that I was a drum major for peace. That I was a drum major for righteousness. And all of the other shallow things will not matter.
—Martin Luther King Jr.

Why am I compelled to write? Because the writing saves me from this complacency I fear. Because I have no choice. Because I must keep the spirit of my revolt and myself alive. Because the world I create in the writing compensates for what the real world does not give me. By writing I put order in the world, give it a handle so I can grasp it.   –Gloria Anzaldúa

Repetition and Parallel Structure

As students read the following paragraph from the famous 1971 essay "Why I Want a Wife" by Judy Syfers Brady, have them identify every use of repetition and parallel structure. In addition, ask them to explain, in a brief paragraph, how the writer uses these structures to build coherence in the paragraph.

> I would like to go back to school so that I can become economically independent, support myself, and, if need be, support those dependent upon me. I want a wife who will work and send me to school. And while I am going to school I want a wife to take care of my children. I want a wife to keep track of the children's doctor and dentist appointments. And to keep track of mine, too. I want a wife to make sure my children eat properly and are kept clean. I want a wife who will wash the children's clothes and keep them mended. I want a wife who is a good nurturant attendant to my children, who arranges for their schooling, makes sure that they have an adequate social life with their peers, takes them to the park, the zoo, etc. I want a wife who takes care of the children when they are sick, a wife who arranges to be around when the children need special care, because, of course, I cannot miss classes at school. My wife must arrange to lose time at work and not lose the job. It may mean a small cut in my wife's income from time to time, but I guess I can tolerate that. Needless to say, my wife will arrange and pay for the care of the children while my wife is working.

Transitional Devices

Read aloud to the class the following selection from Chapter 34 of Charlotte Brontë's *Jane Eyre*. As you read, your students should jot down the transitional devices they hear.

> My first aim will be to *clean down* . . . Moor House from chamber to cellar; my next to rub it up with beeswax, oil, and an indefinite number of cloths, till it glitters again; my third, to arrange every chair, table, bed, carpet, with mathematical precision; afterwards I shall go near to ruin you in coals and peat to keep up good fires in every room; and lastly, the two days preceding that on which your sisters are expected will be devoted by Hannah and me to such a beating of eggs, sorting of currants, grating of spices, compounding of Christmas cakes, chopping up of materials for mince-pies, and solemnising of other culinary rites, as words can convey but an inadequate notion of to the uninitiated like you. My purpose, in short, is to have all things in an absolutely perfect state of readiness for Diana and Mary before next Thursday; and my ambition is to give them a beau-ideal of a welcome when they come.

Diane Belcher, director of the ESL program at Ohio State University, notes that overuse of taxonomies of transitions are of very limited help to multilingual writers, pointing out that such lists may lead students to conclude an essay with "at last" rather than "in conclusion"—*without* humorous or ironic intent (personal correspondence).

Activity: Making Paragraphs Coherent 1—Transitional Devices

Have students break into groups and trade drafts of current essays. As they read one another's papers, they should draw arrows between or circles around key terms, ideas, and pronouns; mark transitional phrases with heavy underlining; and label parallel structures with *//sm*. By stopping to analyze patterns in their writing, students can come to a better understanding of the elements of unity and coherence necessary for constructing effective paragraphs.

Activity: Making Paragraphs Coherent 2—Organization

To give students practice using *spatial order,* suggest that they write about their view of their bedrooms or dorm rooms upon waking. After they record the information, ask them to read their essays to see if they started out or ended up with a controlling idea. Remind them to identify the topic sentence.

To give students practice using *chronological order,* suggest that they write a paragraph about their morning routines. Then ask them to mark the controlling idea. Do they have a topic sentence? Or did they come to one after they wrote the paragraph?

Have students practice using *logical order* by writing a paragraph describing their possessions—academic/personal; from home/from school; old/new; personal/public. They may want to look around their rooms as they write. Did they start out or end up with a controlling idea? What is it? Do they have a topic sentence?

Ask students to attempt a chain of *associations* in order to experiment with this type of organization. Have them study an advertisement from a popular magazine and freewrite a series of sentence fragments in response. Then have them revise their freewriting into a short opinion essay to be submitted to the magazine. When they are done, encourage them to reflect on the process: Did they begin with a strong response and move toward a conclusion? Did they discover unexpected ideas as they wrote? How is the presentation of controlling ideas different in this short opinion piece than in a full-length essay?

Teaching Advice: Linking Paragraphs Together

You might ask students to think of linking paragraphs in terms of the game of dominos. Each paragraph needs to share a similarity with the previous one: just as in dominos, you can only connect two game pieces that have the same number of points on them. Drawing a spatial model of the dominos game on the board for students often helps open their eyes to the way in which writing also works as a series of relationships within and between paragraphs.

Teaching Advice: Writing Special-Purpose Paragraphs

Ask students to bring in magazine articles in which you will highlight the various purposes served by particular paragraphs, especially the introductory and concluding paragraphs. Alert students to the presence and function of transitional paragraphs in especially long prose texts. It is important to stress that of all the paragraphs in a piece of writing, none is more important than the first. In fact, outside of classroom assignments—in job applications, newspaper articles, and fund-raising appeals, for example—the quality of the opening paragraph often determines whether readers bother to read further.

One high school student, Ted Frantz, found himself concentrating hard on his opening paragraph as he worked on a college application essay describing his "major academic interest." Following is the paragraph he came up with to get his readers' attention and introduce his subject.

> Picture a five-year-old boy with a stack of cards in his hands, not baseball cards but presidential flash cards. He would run around asking anybody to question him about presidents; this kid knew incredible facts and could name every president in the correct order from Washington to Bush. I was this little boy, and ever since I was five, I have had a passion for studying history.

Consider asking students to take some time to look at the opening paragraphs in the reading they normally do: newspapers or magazines, textbooks, junk mail, Web sites, and blogs. How well do such paragraphs get and hold their attention? Ask students to bring the paragraphs to class for discussion.

When you are ready to work on conclusions, you will find the following activity helpful.

Activity: Writing Special-Purpose Paragraphs—Conclusions

Ask students to draft three different attempts at concluding their essays. Have them share these samples in writing groups and talk about what works and what doesn't work in each draft. If the essay is only two or three pages in length, you can ask students to read through to the penultimate paragraph and then jot down their thoughts on how best to conclude the essay *before* turning to the three conclusion attempts.

Resources

Section	The St. Martin's Handbook	The Everyday Writer	EasyWriter
Creating Strong Paragraphs	5a	8a	2e
Writing Unified Paragraphs	5b	8a	2e
Developing Paragraphs	5c	8b–8d	2e
Making Paragraphs Coherent	5d	8e	2e
Linking Paragraphs Together	5e	8e	2e
Writing Special Purpose Paragraphs	5f	8f	2e

Note: Depending on which book you are using, student essays may appear online rather than in print. Check the Directory of Student Writing for locations.

Argument

Critical Reading: Overview

One of the primary benefits of teaching students the conventions of academic discourse is that it demonstrates to them the mutual reciprocity between the reading and writing processes. The interconnection between reading and writing has received a great deal of attention during the past decade. It has become clear that writing teachers are doing far more than teaching sentence structure—we are helping to introduce students to a discourse with which many of them are unfamiliar. Standard academic discourse is more than just correctness; it is a style of presentation that involves awareness of audience, grasp of subject, and confidence in the writer's own ethos and abilities. As David Bartholomae says in "Inventing the University,"

> Every time a student sits down to write for us, he has to invent the university for the occasion—invent the university, that is, or a branch of it, like history or anthropology or economics or English. The student has to learn to speak our language, to speak as we do, to try on the peculiar ways of knowing, selecting, evaluating, reporting, concluding and arguing that define the discourse of our community. . . . The student has to appropriate (or be appropriated by) a specialized discourse, and he has to do this as though he were easily and comfortably one with his audience, as though he were a member of the academy or an historian or an anthropologist or an economist; he has to invent the university by assembling and mimicking its language while finding some compromise between idiosyncrasy, a personal history, on the one hand, and the requirements of convention, the history of a discipline, on the other. He must learn to speak our language.

In order to become part of the conversation of academic discourse, students must be exposed to it. Readings in a writing course assist this process in several ways: they provide models of good writing (as well as models of writing to be avoided); they provide content issues that can be discussed; they provide analyses of the decisions that writers have made; and they can illuminate the composing process.

Teaching Advice: Critical Reading

Encourage students to follow the guidelines for critical reading that are listed here for any kind of text, whether written, visual, or a combination of the two. Emphasize that they should employ their critical reading skills when working with digital and new media texts as well.

Guidelines for critical reading

Preview for preliminary questions:

- What does the title tell you?
- What do you already know about the subject?
- What information can you find about the author and his or her expertise or biases?
- What does the time and place of publication tell you?
- What effects do the visuals and headings have?
- What do you expect the main point to be?

Read and annotate the text:

- What key terms and ideas do you identify?
- With which statements do you agree? disagree?
- What sources does the text cite?
- What do you find confusing or unclear?

Summarize what you have read; jot down questions.

Analyze the text:

- Do the main points match your expectations?
- What evidence does the text provide? What counterevidence occurs to you or is missing?
- Are the sources trustworthy?

Then, you can use the following activities for continued practice in previewing, reading, annotating, and analyzing.

Activity: Previewing a Text

To have students develop critical reading skills, ask them to compare the same text in two formats: as a written speech and as a short video of the speech. Visit the American Rhetoric Web site (www.americanrhetoric.com), and select a text to preview using the questions in 7a of *The St. Martin's Handbook*; in the "Start with a Preview" section of the Game Plan, "Read Critically," in Chapter 11 of *The Everyday Writer*; or in the first three bullets of the Checklist, "Guidelines for Critical Reading," in 3a of *EasyWriter*. What do students learn about the author or creator? Is the author different from the speaker in the video? What questions do students have about the subject? Finally, how might students compare the genre of the speech text, which is often found at the bottom of the page, with the performance of the speaker in the video? Use these questions to launch a discussion in class about the importance of reading critically—and how students today need skills in visual and multimedia literacy as well as verbal literacy.

Activity: Reading and Annotating a Text

Building on students' familiarity with the Internet, ask them to work in small groups to identify a favorite Web site. Then have the groups work together through the questions in 7b of *The St. Martin's Handbook*; in the "Read Carefully" section of the Game Plan, "Read Critically," in Chapter 11 of *The Everyday Writer*; or in the "Read and Annotate the Text" section of the Checklist, "Guidelines for Critical Reading," in 3a of *EasyWriter* and prepare to present their findings to the class. One student can take notes about the content questions, a second student can prepare to speak about reading for design and composition, and a third student can make annotations on the Web site after pasting a screen shot of it into a Word document.

Activity: Analyzing a Text

Assign each pair of students a brief text—a letter to the editor or editorial, a school newspaper article, an advertisement, an editorial cartoon, or a blog post. Then ask students to work together to analyze this text using the questions listed in 7d of *The St. Martin's Handbook*; in the "Analyze the Text" section of the Game Plan, "Read Critically," in Chapter 11 of *The Everyday Writer*; or in the sixth through eighth bullets of the Checklist, "Guidelines for Critical Reading," in 3a of *EasyWriter*. Still working together, students should write two or three paragraphs as a group. Gather back together as a class, and have each group read out its work, giving other groups a chance to respond with words of praise or with opposing perspectives on the text.

Analyzing Arguments: Overview

The pervasiveness of argument in our lives makes developing the ability to analyze arguments necessary. This is easier said than done, but the following advice and activities should help you work with students to develop the skills that are essential for adequately addressing arguments: considering contexts, understanding appeals, and identifying fallacies.

Activity: Thinking Critically about Argument

Break the class into groups, and have them answer the following questions as they relate to "A Curse and a Blessing," the student essay by Milena Ateyea.

- What is the writer's agenda—his or her unstated purpose?
- Why does the writer hold these ideas or beliefs? What larger social, economic, political, or other conditions or factors may have influenced him or her?
- What does the writer want readers to do—and why?
- What are the writer's qualifications for making this argument?
- What reasons does the writer offer in support of his or her ideas? Are they good reasons?
- What are the writer's underlying values or unstated assumptions? Are they acceptable—and why, or why not?
- What sources does the writer rely on? How current and reliable are they? What agendas do these sources have? Are any perspectives left out?
- What objections might be made to the argument?

- What individual or group is responsible for publishing or promoting the argument?
- Study the visual and audio aspects of arguments, including the use of color, graphics, and multimedia techniques. How do media and design appeal to the reader or listener? What do they contribute to the argument?

These are the kinds of questions that the group will want to use again and again as they write essays and review the essays of the other group members.

Activity: Considering Cultural Contexts

To foster understanding of how any event or topic has multiple points of view, have the students choose a topic or event as a class. In small groups, students should research and discuss the perspective of a specific cultural group. For example, a discussion of Muslim women's dress code could take the points of view of Islamic scholars, Muslim women, and American feminists, among others. After each group presents its perspective, the class will have a better understanding of the cultural biases and assumptions inherent in arguments.

Activity: Reading Emotional, Ethical, and Logical Appeals 1

To help students identify how word choice can create bias, make two columns on the board labeled "We" and "They." As a class, identify the kinds of words that would be used in each column. For example, We plan/They plot; We are clever/They are sneaky; and so on. You might have them examine editorials, blogs, or other opinion writing to help them recognize such language.

Activity: Reading Emotional, Ethical, and Logical Appeals 2

In order to help students understand Aristotle's three appeals, assign one essay that contains instances of all three types of appeal and form students into three small groups to analyze the presence of each appeal. Jonathan Swift's famous essay "A Modest Proposal" works particularly well for this activity, and many students may already have encountered the essay earlier in their education. If so, they can then serve as content advisers for their small group, explaining the essay's purpose and meaning.

For collaborative work, ask each group to identify passages that make use of one of the appeals (*pathos*, *ethos*, or *logos*) and to comment on the function and efficacy of each appeal in the essay. Each group should provide a short presentation to the class. You might also ask each group to formulate a contemporary argument equivalent to Swift's essay and create a mock appeal for that topic. How might a contemporary writer or politician employ pathos, logos, or ethos to address world hunger? war? AIDS? poverty? Get students to come up with their own analogies and appeals and then share them with the class.

Another, more contemporary, essay that students would have fun analyzing for appeals is Leon Kass's essay, "The End of Courtship." Readily available in three parts, allowing for analysis of shorter or longer pieces, the provocative essay generates much discussion for both traditional and nontraditional students. It can be found on the Webzine Boundless.org. You might also ask students to find recent political essays or speeches to analyze how they employ pathos, logos, or ethos. Suggested topics include world hunger, war, genocide, AIDS, poverty, and the energy crisis. Get students to come up with their own analogies and appeals, and then have them share these with the class.

Activity: Identifying Elements of an Argument

Ask students to analyze Teal Pfeifer's essay about the effect of images in the media on women's perceptions of themselves, reading it now for its implicit argument. Have them analyze the essay using the five Toulmin categories, focusing especially on the assumptions that underlie the writer's claims. Does the essay succeed as an argument? Why or why not?

Teaching Advice: Identifying Fallacies

Writers who rely on manufactured methods of persuasion—distorting evidence, misquoting, misrepresenting opposing views—do not trust their own position on an issue and may not be able to represent that position believably. Encourage students to rely on the strengths of their personal experience as well as the facts they have selected to support their position on an issue. Then, try the following activities.

Activity: Identifying Fallacies 1

Ask students to bring in ads that *do not* fairly represent a product, or an editorial, letter to the editor, or blog post that presents distorted evidence. What are the contexts for the examples? What specifically is slanted or unfair? Then ask students (1) to write out their responses to the examples and (2) to rewrite the ad or example according to fair standards. By doing such analyses, your students will sharpen their critical thinking, reading, and writing skills.

Activity: Identifying Fallacies 2

Instruct the students that they should consider themselves masters of manipulation, and their job is to teach unscrupulous people how to gain influence over others. Then, have the class choose a controversial topic and split the class into two groups—pro and con. Each group of master manipulators should deliberately use as many fallacies as possible (they could think of them as "tricks") to show how to "win" the argument at all costs. Role-playing like this will help them to recognize fallacies more frequently.

Activity: Analyzing Arguments

Ask students to work with one or two classmates and choose a brief argumentative text—whether an essay, advertisement, editorial cartoon, or blog post. Then ask them to work together to analyze the text, playing the believing and doubting game; identifying emotional, ethical, and logical appeals; and listing claims, reasons, assumptions, evidence, and qualifiers.

Finally, ask the groups to collaborate on a two-page double-spaced critical response and present the results of their analysis to the class.

Constructing Arguments: Overview

Argumentation, persuasion, rhetoric—these terms may bring to mind images of hostility, manipulation, deception, and of overpowering, overmastering, and outmaneuvering. In *A Rhetoric of Motives*, Kenneth Burke postulates that the image of persuasion should not be bellicose but rather that

> a speaker persuades an audience by the use of stylistic identifications; his act of persuasion may be for the purpose of causing the audience to identify itself with the speaker's interests; and the speaker draws on identification of interests to establish rapport between himself and his audience.

Identification, Burke reminds us, occurs when people share some principle in common—that is, when they establish common ground. Persuasion should not begin with absolute confrontation and separation but with the establishment of common ground, from which differences can be worked out. Such common ground can help students establish their credibility and understand where their audiences are coming from.

When teaching students how to construct arguments, you may wish to reiterate Burke's emphasis on identification and common ground. At the same time, it is helpful to encourage students to advance their own ideas: as Virginia Woolf notes, "fierce attachment to an idea" makes for powerful writing. This balance of identification and originality might be best understood as contributing a new idea to an ongoing conversation. Teaching thesis statements as beginnings of conversations rather than as statements of finality, D. Diane Davis suggests, emphasizes "the encounter" present in all writing.

Activity: Formulating a Working Thesis

Have students work in small groups to test the following thesis statements for purpose, audience, position, and support:

1. My essay will deal with the issue of recruiting college athletes. My audience is made up of coaches and administrators, and I want to point out that it is their insistence on winning seasons that often causes coaches to resort to unethical recruiting practices.

2. In this essay, I will argue that this university discriminates against people who live off campus and who must drive to school. I know this is true because I am a commuter and can never find a parking spot. If there's a blizzard, the university doesn't close because residence-hall students can walk to class. The university schedules two or three hours between classes for commuter students and then doesn't provide them with any place to go except the library, where you can't even get a soda.

How can these statements be improved? Ask each group of students to provide a revision of one of the statements, working together to formulate a better thesis.

Activity: Shape Your Appeal to Your Audience

Once students have determined their main argument, have them identify two different audiences. Ask them to brainstorm in pairs about the diverse approaches they might take to reach the different audiences. This exercise will help them write an effective argument and will also generate more specific counterarguments.

Teaching Advice: Making Ethical Appeals

Some students may consider it rude or arrogant to advance their own credibility as experts in an area or as originators of an idea. For these students, emphasize that writers can build respect and credibility not simply by demonstrating knowledge through claims of expertise but also in more graceful ways, such as by building common ground, appealing to authority, citing evidence uncovered during the research process, and referring to others who have previously participated in the conversation on the topic at hand. When students focus on making connections with their audience and on building identification rather than animosity, they develop a more collegial, less blatantly aggressive voice that has more persuasive power in an argument.

Fairness toward Counterarguments

POHS EEFFOC—that's "COFFEE SHOP" backwards, when you look through the glass from the other side. Ask students to try to see the point of view of the "opposition" and honestly consider counterarguments. When they try to decipher POHS EEFFOC, they show their willingness to go over to the other side to get a better view of the rhetorical situation. They also demonstrate their developing skills in constructing arguments.

Activity: Making Ethical Appeals—Common Ground

Your students will better understand the concept of common ground if you provide them with an opportunity to demonstrate how opposing parties can reach agreement. Divide the class into pairs of students who hold opposing views, and ask each pair to establish a first principle of agreement, their common ground. Use frustrating situations the students experience or some of the following rhetorical situations:

1. Your roommate keeps an annoying schedule. (For example, if an early bird and a night owl are roommates, they may keep antagonistic schedules. Yet when they discuss their unhappiness, both agree that they each need quiet for sleeping and studying and noise for relaxing. They have thus established common ground, a starting point for working out their differences.)
2. Your English instructor doesn't accept late papers.
3. A member of your group is not pulling his or her weight on your assigned group project.
4. You'd like time off from work to go to Florida during spring break.
5. Your partner constantly borrows your belongings.
6. You need help with child care or household duties.

Teaching Advice: Making Logical Appeals

Students in Western countries often look to logical appeals as *the* most effective way to persuade an audience. Students from math and science backgrounds, steeped in logical positivism, frequently declare that "hard evidence" such as statistics and "concrete logic" such as rational arguments and syllogisms are the only certain modes for convincing an audience. These students may benefit from reading Darrell Huff's *How to Lie with Statistics* and other texts that analyze how scientific information and statistics are manipulated, selected, and presented to an audience using loaded language and claims to authority. In short, teach students that the most persuasive argument does not merely employ logos but rather interweaves Aristotle's three appeals in a strategic crafting of knowledge.

Examples, Precedents, and Narratives

Judith Gardner of the University of Texas at San Antonio warns that college writers can get into trouble through overdependence on stories, and she cautions that writing from sources is not telling a story; narrative should be used to support the point, not *be* the point.

Authority and Testimony

Student writers sometimes rely too heavily on authority figures because they doubt the power of their own strongly held opinions—opinions that might well influence their readers. Encourage your students to cite authorities to support—not substitute for—their own positions on an issue.

While you help students consider the appropriateness and proportion of their use of authority, ask them to consider the authority of celebrities when they tell students to stay in school or appear in other public service announcements. Do students pay any attention to or respect these campaigns? Do they buy hamburgers, athletic shoes, soft drinks, or other products on the advice of the celebrities who endorse them? You might bring in several examples of such celebrity advertisements—from television, print ads, or the Internet—for discussion.

Often students overlook the testimony of ordinary people as a means of identifying with their readers; they don't realize that the testimony of someone with firsthand experience lends powerful credibility to an argument. Although Nancy Reagan conducted a very visible "Just say no to drugs" campaign, her credibility was perhaps not as strong as that of an inner-city resident who had witnessed the effects of the drug trade at close range.

Ask students to identify current celebrities and public figures who are campaigning for a cause, and discuss how their status works for or against their appeal. How do these compare with campaigns that utilize ordinary people? Which type do students find more persuasive and why?

Causes and Effects

Cause-effect relationships are often complex: what appears at first glance to be the obvious cause of an event turns out to be only a secondary influence, sometimes an influence that obscures the primary cause-effect relationship.

For practice, ask students to identify the obvious and not-so-obvious connections in the following statements of cause and effect:

1. A large increase in church membership in recent years shows that people are becoming more religious.

2. Older women sometimes fall and break their hips because they don't consume enough calcium.

3. Because of its elderly population, Florida is the best place to buy a gently used car.

4. Republican victories in nearly every presidential election since 1968 show that the country has repudiated social welfare programs.

Inductive and Deductive Reasoning

One of Aristotle's greatest contributions to rhetorical theory was the use of deductive as well as inductive logic: he used the enthymeme, whose essential difference from the syllogism in logic is not so much that one of the premises is left unstated as that the argument is based on premises that are probably true rather than absolutely true and that the opening premise is agreed on by the speaker and audience. In his analysis of inductive reasoning, Aristotle put great emphasis on the importance of examples.

Most of us live our lives according to inductive generalizations: we are aware of the probability that we will miss the heavy traffic if we take a particular route to school each day; that we can stay in the hot sun only so long without getting burned; that we must eat and exercise a specific amount if we are to stay in shape; or that certain foods, animals, and plants provoke an allergic reaction in us. Many such generalizations stem from inductive reasoning: morning traffic is heavy, sun can burn the skin, consuming too many calories makes one gain weight, poison ivy causes a rash.

Teaching Advice: Making Emotional Appeals

Although emotional appeals have traditionally been ignored or devalued as inappropriate to "good" arguments, they are widely used—and widely effective. For example, some emotional appeals, including bandwagon and various kinds of flattery as well as boasting and exaggeration, are well-known and highly effective appeals characteristic of African American rhetorical strategy. For suggestions on ways of drawing on this rhetorical tradition, see Geneva Smitherman's article "'The Blacker the Berry, the Sweeter the Juice': African American Student Writers." In addition, the following activity will help students understand how visuals are especially effective in appealing to the emotions.

Activity: Making Emotional Appeals—Visuals

Divide the class into small groups, and ask students to find visuals to support an argument for one of the following topics. Have them speculate on what subtopics might be created to support these arguments, write out the working thesis, and then work to construct a set of rough notes for each argument. They should also locate two to three visuals to use as emotional appeals for one of the topics:

1. banning smoking in all public places

2. federal immigration policy

3. "nontraditional" students

4. a topic of current import on campus

Activity: Using Sources in an Argument

You can help students get started on their own arguments by walking them through a "model" example in the computer classroom. Have students choose one of the following statements and make notes on their computers regarding any personal experience they have that supports or refutes the statement. Then have them use library and online sources to gather as much additional evidence as possible. Finally, ask them to use this information and their notes on personal experience to outline a short essay arguing for or against the statement.

1. Vegetarians have a lower incidence of heart attacks than meat-eaters.

2. College degrees lead to higher incomes.

3. To succeed, college students must resort to various forms of dishonesty.

4. Students should graduate from college if only to be four years older and wiser when they join the job market.

5. Exercise relieves stress.

6. We are returning to the moral standards of the fifties.

7. AIDS is the worst disease the United States has ever known.

8. Student loans, grants, and scholarships are becoming scarce.

Project one or two outlines on a large screen for collective class analysis and revision.

Activity: Organizing an Argument

Help clarify the five-part classical argument by providing the class with an essay that follows this format. The "My Turn" column in *Newsweek* is a good choice, as are the editorials in city and campus newspapers or blog posts. Ask students to analyze the essay, identifying the introduction, background, lines of argument, refutation, and conclusion. As you proceed through this exercise, use the board to outline the thesis statement as well as the five major headings. Then have students analyze their own drafts using the same categories.

You can extend this exercise by asking students to find an essay on their own that uses this form of argument and to write a short commentary on the claim.

Resources

Section	The St. Martin's Handbook	The Everyday Writer	EasyWriter
Critical Reading	7a–7e	11a	3a
Previewing a Text	7a	11a	3a
Reading and Annotating a Text	7b	11a	3a
Analyzing a Text	7d	11a	3a
Thinking Critically about Argument	8b	12a	
Considering Cultural Contexts	8c	12b	
Reading Appeals	8d	12c	3c
Identifying Elements of an Argument	8e	12d	3d
Identifying Fallacies	8f	12f	
Formulating a Working Thesis	9c	13b–13c	3e
Shape Your Appeal to Your Audience	9d	13d	3e
Making Ethical Appeals	9e	13e	3e
Making Logical Appeals	9f	13f	3e
Making Emotional Appeals	9g	13g	3e
Using Sources in an Argument	9h	13h	
Organizing an Argument	9i	13i	3f

Note: Depending on which book you are using, student essays may appear online rather than in print. Check the Directory of Student Writing for locations.

Research

Preparing for a Research Project: Overview

The fifteenth edition of the *New Encyclopaedia Britannica* (*NEB*) (1987) attributes the dominance of human beings on earth to the "innate ability to communicate and to store, retrieve, and use knowledge so that each generation does not have to relearn the lessons of the past in order to act effectively in the present." Research is the activity that enables us to process, create, and communicate knowledge. But research goes beyond simply gathering data and passing it on. In its most beneficial sense, research is the process of investigating information or data for a purpose: to make decisions about our lives, to understand our world, or to create or advance understanding. Far from being restricted to work on a college "research essay," research informs much of what we do throughout our lives, especially in the age of electronic media. Research carried out for *The St. Martin's Handbook*, in fact, revealed just how much research students today are doing online for *non*school related uses, from tracking the performance of stocks or sports teams to comparison shopping for a smartphone.

Regardless of the field of study, researching, writing, and learning are interconnected. James Britton's distinction between expressive and trans-actional writing helps explain this interconnection. We write in order to learn; that is, we think on paper, using writing to process information and to probe ideas. This function of writing, a form of self-expression and exploration, Britton calls *expressive*. It serves the writer; it enables him or her to learn and understand information. We also write to communicate learning. We use language to inform, to persuade, or to help someone else understand. This function Britton calls *transactional* to emphasize the exchange or transmission of information for an audience's learning purposes. Similarly, Janet Emig views writing as a means of discovery in which research, writing, and learning are intrinsically connected. She argues that the notes, outlines, and drafts that comprise the research and writing process provide a record of the growth of learning.

Teaching Advice: Considering the Research Process

As preparation for a discussion of the nature and process of college-level research, have students write in their logs about their previous experiences with research (including online research) and research papers. Then, ask your students to share their experiences aloud in class. Use this discussion to build into the following activity.

Activity: Considering the Research Process

Working with one or two members of the class, students should come up with a list of everyday research tasks they have done lately—on what bike or media player to buy, on where to take a vacation, on where to go to college, and so on. Next, the groups should choose two of these everyday research projects and detail their information-gathering processes. All groups should bring the results of their work to share with the class. In your closing discussion of this activity, ask students to identify the steps each group took to find the information they needed. What patterns can the students find among these processes?

Teaching Advice: Analyzing the Assignment

Have students bring in three research assignments from other classes. Use these as the basis for group discussions of the purpose, scope, and audience implied in the assignments.

Identifying the audience will likely pose problems for your students. Answering the questions in this section about audience for each of the research assignments brought in by the groups will help students understand that they must consider the audience when deciding on word choice, tone, strategy, and presentation. Next, ask students to answer the rest of the questions in this section, assessing the rhetorical situation for the assignment.

Point out to your students that one of their responsibilities as researchers and writers is to make information available and understandable to a variety of audiences and in a variety of rhetorical situations. To do so involves making choices about language and development that depend on their analysis of the purpose of the research, the scope of the project or topic, the specific audience, and so on. For example, the physiologist presenting material on limb regeneration should judge how much he or she needs to explain the significance of *blastema* and the relevant aspects of it on the basis of purpose, audience, and scope. Clearly, colleagues in the writer's own field, unlike a general audience, will not require a preliminary basic working definition of the term *blastema*. On the other hand, this physiologist would need to define the term and others particular to the field if the essay were written for an audience made up of readers outside the field.

To help students manage the time line for their assignments, provide them with a sample schedule on your course Web site and ask them to download it to their own computers. Teachers have used technological resources to post a weekly time-check on a course Web site, to offer time-saving tips on the research process and links to time-management workshops on campus, and to use email and discussion forums as a way to submit works in progress.

Teaching Advice: Narrowing a Topic

Ask students to think of an occasion when a question has puzzled or challenged them. Have them jot down ideas about the kind of research they could do to help answer their questions, and then choose one or two examples of such questions to put on the board. Lead the class in a brainstorming session on what kind of research would best help answer these questions.

Finally, ask students to work in small groups to discuss the aspects of their topics that they would like to focus on in their papers. What positions might they take about their chosen topics? How might they select one or two angles or elements to explore? Have them freewrite their responses as they narrow their research topics. You can use this as a segue into the following activity.

Activity: Narrowing a Topic

Have students work in groups of three. Ask them to create some possible research questions on topics and then exchange these with two other groups. Ask the other groups to analyze the topic for the purpose of the research, the audience, the scope, and length limits. This will help each student narrow the topic into a more feasible and focused project.

Activity: Moving from Research Question to Hypothesis

One way of moving students from research questions toward a working hypothesis is to have them brainstorm ways to refine the topic. After students have explored and narrowed their topics using some of the techniques presented earlier, ask them to explain their topics to the class individually. They should briefly explain their interest in the topic, give some background or contextual information, and identify their research question.

Next, open the discussion up to the class. Encourage students to ask questions and to respond to the topic. By fielding the class's questions and responses, students will develop a sense of the possible directions their topics can take. This informal class brainstorming session can help them identify perspectives that interest others in the topic. By the end of the session, in response to the student questions, the speakers can have generated a working hypothesis—their stance on the issue.

Limit each student's individual session to fifteen minutes—five minutes for the student to present his or her topic, and ten minutes for the class to respond and ask questions. At the end of the fifteen minutes, have each student freewrite for ten to fifteen minutes, noting (1) suggestions for focusing, narrowing, or phrasing the research question; (2) a statement or working hypothesis on his or her own interest in or possible approach to the topic; or (3) remarks on matters of purpose, audience, scope, or length.

To make the most of the activity, have at least four individual sessions, with no more than two topics presented in any one class. Then break up the class into groups of four or five to work through this activity. The small-group activity gives the entire class practice at working out possible topics.

Teaching Advice: Making a Preliminary Research Plan

Scientist and writer Lewis Thomas recommended taking alternate routes to exploring a question or research topic, including going in the opposite direction from what seems most natural or just "fiddling around." "Fiddle around," he said, ". . . but never with ways to keep things the same, no matter who, not even yourself." As students begin to formulate a preliminary research plan, encourage them to "fiddle around" as part of the process.

You can provide students with a sample schedule on your course Web site and ask them to download it to their own research files. Alternatively, keep a class time line on your Web site and update it weekly to show your collective progress in meeting the class research deadlines. Since one of the main challenges students have with research projects is managing their time, requiring students to check in electronically on a regular basis helps them keep up with the process. It also gives you an opportunity to regularly post time-saving tips on the research process and links to time-management workshops on campus, and to use email and discussion forums as a means of submission for works in progress.

Teaching Advice: Keeping a Research Log

A research log (or a section of the writing log set off for such a purpose) is a good place to keep track of reading, note-taking, and writing progress; to ask questions; and to formulate tentative syntheses or conclusions. But no less important, it is a good place to write about the blocks, obstacles, or challenges any researcher inevitably faces. Point out these uses to your students, and ask them to make several log entries on their research processes. You can use these as the basis for class discussions on how to make research most efficient and productive.

Students are often hungry to learn practical and successful methods for completing the research process. Suggest to them that they work directly with technology as they begin the research process and construct their research logs. When they are exploring library databases online, they can cut and paste citation information right into a working bibliography. If they find potentially useful quotations or images, they should attach the source information below the copied text. Some students even download articles from large databases such as FirstSearch, LexisNexis, EBSCOhost, and Medline in order to cite materials. If you require students to hand in copies of all works cited and consulted, allowing electronic versions can save both time and trees.

Teaching Advice: Moving from Hypothesis to Working Thesis

As students work on their research projects, remind them that their focus and working hypotheses will naturally shift. Share with them stories about famous researchers who might serve as role models.

In the following passage, for example, astronomer Carl Sagan describes the excitement of the kind of research in which he is engaged, research that makes you "really think" and consequently "experience a kind of exhilaration." Ask students to read Sagan's description carefully. Have they done any research that fits his description? What kind of research would allow them to experience "exhilaration"? How might their own research process develop in this way?

> . . . the main trick of [doing research in] science is to *really* think of something: the shape of clouds and their occasional sharp bottom edges at the same altitude everywhere in the sky; the formation of a dewdrop on a leaf; the origin of a name or a word—Shakespeare, say, or "philanthropic"; the reason for human social customs—the incest taboo, for example; how it is that a lens in sunlight can make paper burn; how a "walking stick" got to look so much like a twig; why the Moon seems to follow us as we walk; what prevents us from digging a hole down to the center of the Earth; what the definition is of "down" on a spherical Earth; how it is possible for the body to convert yesterday's lunch into today's muscle and sinew; or how far is up—does the universe go on forever, or if it does not, is there any meaning to the question

of what lies on the other side? Some of these questions are pretty easy. Others, especially the last, are mysteries to which no one even today knows the answer. They are natural questions to ask. Every culture has posed such questions in one way or another. Almost always the proposed answers are in the nature of "Just So Stories," attempted explanations divorced from experiment, or even from careful comparative observations.

But the scientific cast of mind examines the world critically as if many alternative worlds might exist, as if other things might be here which are not. Then we are forced to ask why what we see is present and not something else. Why are the Sun and the Moon and the planets spheres? Why not pyramids, or cubes, or dodecahedra? Why not irregular, jumbly shapes? Why so symmetrical, worlds? If you spend any time spinning hypotheses, checking to see whether they make sense, whether they conform to what else we know, thinking of tests you can pose to substantiate or deflate your hypotheses, you will find yourself doing science. And as you come to practice this habit of thought more and more you will get better and better at it. To penetrate into the heart of the thing—even a little thing, a blade of grass, as Walt Whitman said—is to experience a kind of exhilaration that, it may be, only human beings of all the beings on this planet can feel. We are an intelligent species and the use of our intelligence quite properly gives us pleasure. In this respect the brain is like a muscle. When we think well, we feel good. Understanding is a kind of ecstasy. 　　　　　　　　　　　　　　　　　　　–Carl Sagan, *Broca's Brain*

Conducting Research: Overview

According to Charles Bazerman in *The Informed Writer*, "gathering convincing data is not easy." The method that a researcher uses greatly determines the evidence that supports the research, the conclusions the researcher is able to draw, and ultimately the effectiveness with which the research will influence others to accept its claims. In other words, the way a researcher explores and produces data will affect how an audience responds to the research.

Will it be believable? Is it accurate? reasonable and reliable? thorough? careful? appropriate? significant? Bazerman advises researchers that "method is so central to the understanding and evaluation of the final written product that in many disciplines a writer is obliged to describe as part of the statement the method used to produce and analyze the data. In this way, many articles contain stories of how they were made."

To appreciate the importance of choosing the methods appropriate to different research projects, researchers need to know that methods vary across disciplines and within them, and that they often change with time. For example, in linguistics, many sociolinguists believe that understanding the way words change in meaning is most accurately explained by observing the way words are used in different social contexts. Historical linguists, on the other hand, prefer to explain meaning changes in terms of the historical origins of words and language groups.

The issue of method is especially important today, as many students are conducting research online. They need to understand the disadvantages as well as the advantages of such research methods. Researchers, for instance, are in some ways at the mercy of whatever search engine they are using: What are its principles of exclusion and inclusion? Discussing these difficult issues in class will pay off—for you as well as for your students.

Teaching Advice: Differentiating Kinds of Sources

Have your students list the sources of information they would use to help a reader decide on which mobile phone plan to choose. They will probably mention their own experiences or their family's experience with a reliable or unreliable service provider. They will probably mention consumer guides. They'll also likely mention newspaper and television advertisements as well as pertinent Web sites. Have them classify these sources as either primary or secondary and explain their classifications.

For example, students' own experiences can be classified as a primary source. The fact that they have used a particular service for many years and that they have recommended it to relatives and friends who have had trouble-free experiences is a form of raw data. If they mention an article that praises their phone plan, the magazine is a secondary source. You can use this as a jumping-off point for the following group activity.

Activity: Differentiating Kinds of Sources

Ask students to work in groups of three and draw up a list of reference sources that would be relevant for the following topics. Then ask them to choose one topic, go to the library, and, using both online and print sources, find the necessary facts. Have them write a brief summary, noting where they found the facts and what strategy they used to do so.

1. the top ten scorers in the WNBA in 2005
2. the articles on Epstein-Barr syndrome published in 1999
3. a description of the elements of deconstructive architecture
4. information on the 2006 Winter Olympics
5. reviews of Susan Sontag's book *On Photography*
6. all the critical articles on Toni Morrison's *Beloved* published between 1990 and 1997
7. information on the life of Gloria Steinem
8. a description of the progress of AIDS research
9. information on Michael Badnarik, the Libertarian presidential candidate in the 2004 election
10. the ten most-often-cited articles on superconductivity in 2000

Teaching Advice: Using the Library to Get Started

As you prepare to introduce your students to the value of using the library for getting started on a research project, you might spend a little time discussing with the class the history of information systems. When the inventions of writing and paper enabled people to accumulate information, efforts were made to keep and present the new written information. Constructed in about 600 BCE, the royal library at Nineveh, capital of the Assyrian empire, may have been among the world's first great libraries. Historians and archaeologists believe that it contained tens of thousands of works on the arts, the sciences, and religion. Its grand achievement of cataloging all contemporary knowledge made it the early ancestor of today's information systems and scientific databases.

Set up a meeting for your class with a reference librarian, or ask a librarian to attend your class, in order to discuss the resources in your particular library and how best for students to get access to them. At many schools, reference librarians are prepared to do a demonstration of online searches for your students as well as provide an overview of the library. Planning a special class session devoted to using the library early on will benefit students throughout the term.

Teaching Advice: Finding Library Resources

Encourage students to explore the range of resources available in the library. Spend some time discussing the differences between online library resources that an institution pays for by subscription—such as JSTOR, FirstSearch, Project Muse, and LexisNexis—and other, less academic and unregulated search engines such as Google.

If you are teaching in a technology-enhanced classroom, you can take advantage of the computers available to you by walking students through interactive exercises in finding library resources. Specifically, ask students to conduct research with different kinds of searches. Put them into groups of three, and have them brainstorm together on the best keywords to use in a database search on the following topics: computer viruses, white-collar crime, contemporary rap, sexual harassment in the military, upcoming NASA missions, and the cost of a college education.

Ask each group to go online and collaboratively find the three most promising sources for their topic. Have each group repeat this exercise with the library's catalog, a subscription database, a book index, a review index, and an e-journal catalog or periodical index. At the end of class, have each group give a five-minute oral presentation on the benefits and disadvantages of each method. Have students write up a short reflection on their investigations into library resources and add this reflection to their research files. The following activity should also be helpful in teaching students how to find library resources.

Activity: Finding Library Resources

To help students understand library resources, ask them to join one or two classmates and pay a visit to the main library on your campus. The team should bring back answers to the following questions: How are the library's materials organized? What resources can you use to find out what your library owns and where these materials are located? What electronic encyclopedias, indexes, and databases are available? What electronic journal collections does your library subscribe to? Each team should write up a brief report that answers these questions and comment on those aspects of the library that the group found most interesting or helpful, most confusing or difficult to use. Review the reports in a larger class discussion.

Teaching Advice: Conducting Internet Research

While most students are now producing their college assignments on computers, and most students are comfortable using the Internet, most still need solid instruction in how to harness the Internet for academic research purposes. Your students need to know how to determine which information is reliable and how to conduct effective searches for their topics. For these reasons, you may want to work through this section with your students, implementing the suggestions for tracking searches and bookmarking useful sites, exploring various search engines with the same set of keywords, and exploring authoritative sources such as the Library of Congress. Try searching in diverse locations with the same set of keywords, and make note of the findings. (See the cross-reference chart on page 120.)

Arrange for a workshop to take place in a computer lab, where students can work online together to conduct some preliminary research. Alternatively, ask if someone in the library or at a public computing site could help you set up such a workshop. Then lead students through a simple search, showing them how to apply the "rules" of various search engines and how to evaluate what they find on the Web. Realize that some students in your class can probably serve as facilitators. This will create a strong community and enable students to learn from one another.

Emphasize that popular texts found on the Web may not necessarily be bad, depending on the purpose of the search and the nature of the assignment. To analyze the marketing strategies of rap artists, for instance, Google might produce better results than LexisNexis.

Teaching Advice: Conducting Field Research

Students may believe that they will simply "get the facts" when they observe and that they will not or do not bring their own interpretive frames to observation. Students in one class, for instance, decided to spread out across campus and observe instances of graffiti, taking notes on their observations. This task seemed very straightforward to them. They soon realized, however, that recording the graffiti out of context changed it in significant ways. These examples of graffiti—perhaps scrawled in giant letters sideways on a door—just didn't mean the same thing when printed neatly in a notebook. Nor did the students record their observations in the same ways, or even with the same consistency. In this case, the very act of writing down the data changed its context. So the students decided to try to capture something of the spatial orientation and surrounding context of the graffiti by copying the form as well as the content and noting other contextual details. As a result, their data were much richer and more multidimensional than before. You might wish to share this example with students and ask them to talk in class about how they themselves affect the data they gather. In addition, the activities below should help students develop their interviewing and surveying skills.

Observation

Suggest that most students assume the role of reporter, using the *who, what, when, where, why*, and *how* questions to note down what they see and hear. At least in the trial run, these questions can help guide students' observation.

Activity: Conducting Field Research 1—Interviews

Ask students to work in pairs, first preparing tentative interview questions and then practicing these questions on their partners. Each partner, in turn, provides a critique of the questions. As an alternative, set up one mock interview for your class. Then lead a class discussion on the strengths and weaknesses of the interview.

For additional practice, ask students to choose a professor in a field of study that interests them and interview that person about the research the professor tends to do. Encourage them to draw up a list of questions they would like answered about the kind of research questions asked in that field, the most typical methods of answering them, and the kinds of sources most often used. After the interview, have students summarize in two or three paragraphs what they have learned.

Use their findings for a class discussion on how to conduct an effective interview, on the etiquette of interviewing, and on the ethics of interviewing (whether to change a subject's words to correct a "mistake," for example).

Activity: Conducting Field Research 2—Surveys

Though you will often assign research to be carried out individually, you might ask students to work in teams on a project in order to conduct field research in the form of a survey of their peers or of members of their community.

As one possibility, have students work in research teams to gather information for a report on the condition, the level of use, and any needed changes of the bike paths (or commuter parking lots) on campus. Allow a week or so for them to organize their efforts and to decide what kind of survey they will need to do. Have them identify the target audience, generate a list of survey questions, and decide on a method of recording the data (paper survey, Web-based questionnaire, microphone, video recorder). Then ask them to write together a brief summary of how they have proceeded, noting problems they have encountered and projecting ways to solve them.

Evaluating Sources and Taking Notes: Overview

In ordinary language, we say we have received information when *what we know* has changed. The bigger the change in what we know, the more information we have received. Information, like energy, does work. But whereas energy does physical work, information does logical work. While this view that increased information changes what we know is largely true, it's intellectually disastrous to accept blindly and unquestioningly our information sources. A judicious, practiced researcher learns that not everything she or he reads in journals, magazines, scholarly books, or blogs is true simply because it appears in a text. The truly inquisitive researcher understands that no source is totally beyond dispute.

Teaching Advice: Using Sources to Meet a Need

To help students understand what factors determine their decisions for using one source rather than another, ask them to look for biases in the sources they consult in their research areas. Is there such a thing as an unbiased source? If not, why use sources? What purpose do they serve? Challenge students to consider the merits of evaluating and selecting a number of authoritative sources on their topic to widen the scope of their research. By using a range of carefully chosen perspectives, students can broaden and extend the research questions and offer a new contribution to the ongoing conversation.

Activity: Using Sources to Meet a Need

Ask students to work with one or two members of class for this collaborative activity. Each group should read the following passage, in which MIT psychologist Sherry Turkle questions whether the state of flux in which we now live may be not a transitional stage but a permanent feature of our existence. Then discuss why the writer may have used each one of the sources cited. What purpose does each source serve? Bring the results of the group analysis to class for discussion.

> As we stand on the boundary between the real and the virtual, our experience recalls what anthropologist Victor Turner termed a liminal moment, a moment of passage when new cultural symbols and meanings can emerge. Liminal moments are times of tension, extreme reactions, and great opportunity. In our time, we are simultaneously flooded with predictions of doom and predictions of imminent utopia. We live in a crucible of contradictory experience. When Turner talked about liminality, he understood it as a transitional state—but living with flux may no longer be temporary. Donna Haraway's characterization of irony illuminates our situation: "Irony is about contradictions that do not resolve into larger wholes[. . .] about the tension of holding incompatible things together because both or all are necessary and true."
>
> –Sherry Turkle, *Life on the Screen*

Teaching Advice: Keeping a Working Bibliography

You can get students to begin to evaluate sources even as they initially construct a list of sources that seem promising for use in their project. Ask students to record all the source information and a brief description of the writer's bias toward the topic.

Many students, especially those in the sciences, will deny that the author's or researcher's perspective influences research. In science, they may claim, researchers look at phenomena objectively, without interpretive bias. Scientists let the facts and data speak for themselves. Though the bias may not be apparent in the analysis of the data, the conclusions cannot avoid some degree of bias. Conclusions result from the interpretive analysis of data.

For a striking example, see Anne Fausto-Sterling's *Myths of Gender: Biological Theories about Women and Men*. Fausto-Sterling, a biologist, demonstrates that many of the questionable distinctions between males and females that scientists have "proven" derive from their research methods and the kinds of questions they have asked. For instance, male superiority in athletic performance can be "proven" when it is measured by muscle strength rather than other criteria such as resiliency or endurance.

Have students reflect on this example and attempt to notice the bias—or types of questions most interesting to the writer—for each source they consult in their research project and construct an annotated bibliography of sources. Make sure students aim for a balanced list of sources that reflects a wide range of perspectives.

Teaching Advice: Evaluating Usefulness and Credibility

Reading through sources with one's research question in mind is the ideal way of reading with focused efficiency. However, students do not always have a research question in mind when they start. If students haven't formulated one, encourage them to look through the table of contents of several sources on a general topic for a perspective or subheading for potential research subjects.

Before they begin to skim through, they might ask themselves a question about the topic based on the subheadings in the table of contents.

In "The Web Demands Critical Thinking by Students," Kari Boyd McBride and Ruth Dickstein remind instructors that students no longer get most materials for research writing from traditionally reputable print sources available in the library. Because the Web is awash in all kinds of undifferentiated material—some junk, some masterful—we have a special obligation to focus on critical reading, writing, and thinking. To carry out this goal, McBride and Dickstein use an exercise asking students to research a topic using a number of different sources—a book, an article, a reference work, a work identified through use of a CD-ROM index, and a Web site. Students then report on one of these resources, "summarizing the information it contains and evaluating the reliability of the author and the plausibility of the argument." While the authors created the exercise to help students think critically about electronic sources, they found that it had a much wider payoff: it has shown students that even encyclopedia articles can be biased and has led them to look closely at a writer's sources and to ask what makes an argument authoritative and persuasive, whether in print or online. Why not develop and use a similar exercise with your students? Remind students not to underestimate the value of an index. Skimming the index can give students a sense of the depth of information the book includes about a topic and can also give them ideas for different approaches.

Activity: Reading and Interpreting Sources

Ask students to read the following two passages about the War of 1812, the first from an American encyclopedia and the second from a Canadian history book. Have students read each one carefully, with a critical eye, and then answer the following interpretative questions, noting any differences in the two accounts:

1. What motivated the War Hawks?
2. Who attacked whom at the beginning of the Battle of Tippecanoe?
3. What did the War of 1812 mean in British, American, and Canadian history?
4. Why did the Treaty of Ghent end up restoring the prewar boundaries?

Then ask students to answer these questions about both passages:

1. What is the perspective, tone, and argument of each passage?
2. How does each passage make clear its point of view?
3. Can you find at least one example in each passage that seems to show how the author's point of view accounts for or affects the interpretation of events?
4. Why do you think each passage takes the view it does?
5. How would you, as a researcher, evaluate and use these sources?

Have students compare their own critical reading and interpretation with those of other students in your class, and remind them to be prepared for a full class discussion.

From the *World Book Encyclopedia*

The War of 1812

The War of 1812 was in many ways the strangest war in United States history. It could well be named the War of Faulty Communication. Two days before war was declared, the British Government had stated that it would repeal the laws which were the chief excuse for fighting. If there had been telegraphic communication with Europe, the war might well have been avoided. Speedy communication would also have prevented the greatest battle of the war, which was fought at New Orleans fifteen days after a treaty of peace had been signed.

It is strange also that the war for freedom of the seas began with the invasion of Canada, and that the treaty of peace which ended the war settled none of the issues over which it had supposedly been fought.

The chief United States complaint against the British was interference with shipping. But New England, the great shipping section of the United States, bitterly opposed the idea of going to war. The demand for war came chiefly from the West and South, although these sections were not really hurt by British naval policy.

When we add that both sides claimed victory in the War of 1812, it becomes clear that the whole struggle was a confused mass of contradictions. These must be explained and cleared up before we can understand why the democratic United States sided with Napoleon I, the French dictator, in a struggle for world power. . . .

The War Hawks. A group of young men known as "War Hawks" dominated Congress during this period. Henry Clay of Kentucky and John C. Calhoun of South Carolina were the outstanding leaders of the group. Clay was then Speaker of the House of Representatives. Like Clay and Calhoun, most of the War Hawks came from western and southern states, where many of the people were in favor of going to war with Great Britain.

The people of New England generally opposed going to war, because war with Great Britain would wipe out entirely the New England shipping trade which had already been heavily damaged. Another reason New England opposed war was because many New Englanders sympathized with Great Britain in its struggle against the dictator Napoleon.

Many historians believe that a leading motive of the War Hawks was a desire for expansion. The people of the Northwest were meeting armed resistance in their attempt to take more land from the Indians, and they believed that the Indians had considerable British support. An American army was attacked by Indians at the Battle of Tippecanoe in the Wabash Valley in November, 1811, and British guns were found on the battlefield. The Westerners, therefore, were anxious to drive the British out of Canada. Southerners looked longingly at Florida, which belonged to Great Britain's ally, Spain. The South had also suffered a serious loss of markets. But the deciding motive for war seems to have been a strong desire for more territory.

Progress of the War

Declaration of War. On June 1, 1812, President Madison asked Congress to declare war against Great Britain. He gave as his reasons the impressment of United States seamen and the interference with United States trade. He charged also that the British had stirred up Indian warfare in the Northwest. Congress declared war on June 18, 1812. Two days earlier, the British Foreign Minister had announced that the Orders in Council would be repealed, but word of this announcement did not reach America until after the war had begun.

Because President Madison asked for the declaration of war, many Federalists blamed him for the conflict, calling it "Mr. Madison's war." But it was more the War Hawks' war than it was Madison's. . . .

Treaty of Ghent. The British public was tired of war and especially of war taxes. The British Government therefore proposed discussing terms. Commissioners of the two countries met at Ghent, Belgium, in August, 1814.

The British at first insisted that the United States should give up certain territory on the northern frontier, and set up a large permanent Indian reservation in the Northwest. But American victories in the summer and fall of 1814 led the British to drop these demands. A treaty was finally signed on December 24, 1814, in Ghent, Belgium. By its terms, all land which had been captured by either party was to be given up. Everything was to be exactly as it was before the war, and commissions from both of the countries were to settle any disputed points about boundaries. Nothing whatever was said in the treaty about impressments, blockades, or the British Orders in Council, which supposedly had caused the war. The treaty was formally ratified on February 17, 1815.

Results of the War

One important result of the War of 1812 was the rapid rise of manufacturing in the United States. During the war, United States citizens were unable to import goods from Great Britain, and had to begin making many articles for themselves. The war also increased national patriotism, and helped to unite the United States into one nation.

The war settled none of the issues over which the United States had fought. But most of these issues faded out during the following years. In the long period of peace after 1815, the British had no occasion to make use of impressments or blockades. Indian troubles in the Northwest were practically ended by the death of the chief Tecumseh and by the British surrender of Detroit and other posts. The United States occupied part of Florida during the war, and was soon able to buy the rest of it from Spain.

One indirect result of the War of 1812 was the later election to the Presidency of Andrew Jackson and of William Henry Harrison. Both of these men won military fame which had much to do with their elections. Another indirect result was the decline of Federalist power. New England leaders, most of them Federalists, met secretly in Hartford, Conn., to study amendments to the Constitution. Their opponents charged that they had plotted treason, and the Federalists never recovered. . . .

Chief Battles of the War

The War of 1812 was not an all-out struggle on either side. For the British, the war was just an annoying part of their struggle with Napoleon. For many Americans, it was an unjustified attempt to gratify the expansionist ambitions of the South and West.

From *Canada: A Story of Challenge*

Danger on the Western Border

From the Treaty of Versailles in 1783 until the outbreak of a second war with the United States in 1812, the western border of young Canada was never secure. Trouble arose in the lands south of the Great Lakes; in the Ohio country which had been officially granted to the United States in 1783, but which had remained tied to the St Lawrence fur trade. The final consequence was open war. The trouble began almost with the signing of peace in 1783, when Britain quickly came to regret the ready surrender of so much of the West, and sought at least to delay its transfer to the United States.

The chief reasons for delay arose from the fur traders and the Indians who were still the masters of the unsettled Ohio West. The Canadian fur merchants of the St Lawrence drew most of their trade from that country, and they asked that the transfer be postponed for two years until they could adjust their business to this heavy loss. The Indians supplied the major reason, however. They declared that they had been ignored in the Treaty of Versailles and that Britain had handed over their lands, which they had never ceded, to the United States. There was danger that if the West was transferred and opened to American settlement the Indians would, in revenge, attack the thinly held and almost unprotected British settlements in Upper Canada.

Taking advantage of vague wording in the peace treaty, therefore, the British held on to the military and trading posts in the West below the Lakes, giving as their reason the failure of the Americans to carry out the term of the treaty that called for the restoration of Loyalist property. It was a sound reason, but not the chief one for failing to transfer the West.

This situation dragged on into the 1790's, while the Americans feared that the British were arousing the Indians against them, and the British feared that the Indians would become aroused. Dorchester, as governor, darkly expected a new war with the United States, and had some hope of building an Indian state in the Ohio country that would stand between the Americans and the Upper Canadian frontier and help to protect the latter. The Americans, meanwhile, were pressing forward from the region south of the Ohio, and sending forces against the Indians in order to break their hold on the western country. In 1794 one of these expeditions completely defeated the tribes at the battle of Fallen Timbers, and hope of an Indian "buffer state" collapsed. The tribes ceded their lands to the United States. . . .

The rapidly advancing western states of the American union made good use of the growing warlike spirit in the republic. They held that the place to punish Britain was in Canada. Filled with the forceful confidence and expansive drive of the frontier they wanted to add Canada to the American union: a Canada which American frontier settlement had already invaded. Was not Upper Canada by now practically an American state? The "war hawks" of the American West clamoured for an easy conquest. Their chance seemed to arrive in 1811.

In that year the western Indians, being steadily pushed back by advancing American settlement, attempted a last stand. Led by the chief Tecumseh, they formed a league to resist further inroads. The Americans saw this as the threat of a new Pontiac uprising, of savage

Indian raids on the frontier. They attacked the Indians, and by their victory at the battle of Tippecanoe, destroyed Tecumseh's league. Yet the American West was not satisfied. It was fully convinced that the British had been behind the Indians, although the Canadian government had actually sought to keep the Indian league at peace. It seemed that the West would only be safe when the British had been driven out of Canada. The war hawks cried for blood, the American frontier wanted new lands to conquer, and the American East was newly aroused by fresh skirmishes over the right of search. The United States declared war in June, 1812, and set out to capture Canada.

The Second Struggle with the Americans

The War of 1812 in British history is only a side-show, not altogether successful, during the huge and victorious contest with Napoleon. In United States history it is a second war of independence, chiefly against the weight of British sea-power. In Canadian history it is above all a land war, a second struggle against American invasion. All these pictures are partly true; and in studying the Canadian version one must bear in mind that it portrays only the War of 1812 as it affected Canada. Yet for Canada the war was vitally important; far more important than it was for Britain, and much more dangerous than it was for the United States. . . .

Thus the war ended late in 1814 in a stalemate, which was probably a good thing for future peace.

It was not completely a stalemate. Britain still held the West and some of the Maine coast, and the British naval blockade was strangling American commerce. But in the peace negotiations the Americans made clear their readiness to go on fighting rather than yield territory. Faced with a revival of Napoleon's power in Europe at that very moment, Britain did not press the point. As a result the Treaty of Ghent of 1814 simply stopped the fighting, restored the pre-war boundaries, and said little about the problems that had caused the conflict.

Nevertheless in the next few years many of these problems disappeared. The question of the right of search ended with the Napoleonic Wars, and vanished in the long years of peace after 1815. The Indian problem declined as American settlement filled in the old West; the tribes had been too weakened by the war to offer any further resistance. The American war-hawks had found Canada no willing mouthful, and the United States was turning away to expand in a new direction, towards the south. . . .

The War of 1812 thus tended to bring British North America together and strengthened the bond with Britain. Any common feelings among the colonists, however, were largely directed against the United States. This anti-American spirit was still a narrow basis on which to build a Canadian nationalism. Anti-Americanism was particularly evident in Upper Canada. Further American settlement was largely prevented there, and American settlers already in the province were in danger of persecution—the Loyalists' case in reverse—if their declarations of British sentiments were not loud enough. Nevertheless, on the whole these reactions to the strain of the War of 1812 were understandable; and not an extreme price to pay for the survival of British North America.

—J. M. S. Careless

Activity: Synthesizing Sources 1

Ask students to work in small groups and share their responses to the preceding passages about the War of 1812. Then have them synthesize the data and arguments presented by the readings. When students are satisfied that they have captured the main point of each passage, ask them to reflect on their syntheses, drawing out implications and points for discussion. Finally, ask them to work together to develop an interpretation of these sources that all members of the group can agree on. Have them present this synthesis to the class.

Activity: Synthesizing Sources 2

To teach students how to begin synthesizing their material, ask them to keep a record of the main points that emerge from their research about their topic. Under each point, have them make two columns: "similar/agree" and "contrast/disagree." A brief note with the similar or contrasting perspectives and the respective source for each one will allow them to start seeing the bigger picture of how their sources engage one another.

Teaching Advice: Taking Notes and Annotating Sources

Suggest to students that they use the following process when photocopying or downloading research materials:

1. Photocopy or download only the most important material, after reading and selecting it.
2. Highlight essential passages.
3. Quote, paraphrase, or summarize those passages on note cards.
4. Remember to ask permission to use material found on the Internet.

Electronic Note-Taking

Students can save precious time during the research process by taking notes and composing annotations right on a laptop or other computer. Remind students to list the complete information for each source and to provide quotations in full. Have them follow the guidelines in this section. (See the cross-reference chart on page 120.)

Quotations

The cut-and-paste operation of any word-processing program can be extremely helpful in taking down quotations from a source. However, with this ease comes great danger of plagiarism. Make sure that you remind students to follow the example of David Craig's research shown throughout the chapters on research, in attributing the full source and page number for any quotation. Students might also take a moment to describe the context for the quotation and indicate how—and where—they hope to use the quotation in their final paper.

Paraphrases

Paraphrasing is a skill that has twofold value. It helps us communicate, but it also helps us do something else that isn't always readily apparent to students: it helps us in our learning. Because a paraphrase requires us to put someone else's meaning into our own words, we have to understand the meaning of the original. If we have trouble with the paraphrase, our difficulty likely indicates that we don't have an adequate grasp of the original passage. The measure of how well we understand what we've read is the paraphrase (or the summary). In expressing our understanding we are involved in a process of learning.

For this reason, the importance of paraphrasing cannot be overestimated. As students take paraphrase notes in their research logs, make sure to point out the following to them:

1. Often a paraphrase may seem to make sense to the writer, but it may not to a reader because of the writer's familiarity with the original passage and because the paraphrase is in his or her choice of language.
2. There are at least two purposes of paraphrasing, one to help the writer himself or herself understand and another to present the information to another person to understand.
3. Much research involves paraphrasing or explaining ideas in the researcher's own words.

4. Having others respond to their writing helps writers learn how to judge and use language for audiences that are different in their levels of understanding and expertise with a subject.

5. The paraphraser is in some ways always in danger of misrepresenting another, or of satirizing or even parodying another, by taking meanings out of context. Thus, like summaries and quotations, paraphrases should be used with care.

Activity: Taking Notes and Annotating Sources 1—Paraphrase

Whenever students paraphrase, have them compare versions and explain similarities and differences. Collaborating on a second version will help them appreciate not simply where their troubles lie but also the learning effectiveness of collaboratively talking out, working out, and writing out material they are studying.

For additional practice with paraphrasing, divide the class into groups of six, and present them with these instructions: choose for paraphrasing a short passage of about one hundred words from a text, an essay, or an article. Each member of the group should first individually restate the original in his or her own words. Keep in mind that the paraphrase requires a writer to include all major and supporting details. Once they have produced their paraphrases, have them break into three groups of two, and, working together, cowrite a paraphrase of the original excerpt. Then they should discuss the similarities or differences among the three versions. Ask students to try to explain them, especially the differences, focusing on the following guiding questions:

1. Working in pairs, did you disagree over terms and their meaning in the original passage?

2. Was it easy to agree on synonyms or on paraphrases of ideas and concepts?

3. Did you agree on the information to include? to leave out?

4. How similar are the three coauthored versions? How might you account for the differences?

5. What does trying to agree on a paraphrase tell you about how different people read and interpret a passage? about how they choose to rephrase it?

Activity: Taking Notes and Annotating Sources 2—Summary

Have students work in pairs to prepare a paraphrase of a short article. Then have each pair prepare a one- or two-sentence summary of the article, making sure not to plagiarize. Have students bring their paraphrases and summaries to class for discussion.

Integrating Sources into Your Writing: Overview

The process of integrating sources into your writing can be similar to hosting a conversation at a stimulating dinner party. As the dialogue unfolds, various participants have the chance to contribute. But the writer remains the moderator, orchestrating the ebb and flow of conversation. Deciding how and when a source should enter this dialogue is a skill developed best through practice, observation of successful models, and attention to rhetorical purpose. Invite your students to begin the conversation, and look to this chapter for advice on how best to guide them through this process.

While teaching integration of sources, do not discount the importance of helpful examples. Stuart Swirsky, in a review of Candace Spigelman's *Across Property Lines: Textual Ownership in Writing Groups*, stresses the way in which models can lead students toward mastery of complex writing processes such as integrating sources:

> As any writing instructor well knows, a co-requisite to becoming a competent writer is to engage in a tremendous amount of careful and critical reading. Perhaps more than anything else, what students really need is more models for writing, models that are readily available in texts. Getting students to do more reading may be as important as getting them to open up to more collaboration in the classroom.

Activity: Deciding Whether to Quote, Paraphrase, or Summarize

Ask students working in pairs to select an article from a major journal in a field of interest to them. Have them identify each occurrence of paraphrase, summary, or quotation and the function that each serves. These may include:

1. to provide background information
2. to define terms
3. to provide a position for rebuttal
4. to explain quoted material
5. to illustrate a point
6. to show disagreements among sources
7. to cite authorities and, hence, to reinforce claims, statements, or credibility
8. to state a point more precisely, powerfully, or accurately than with a paraphrased version
9. to challenge, resist, or even parody the source

Once two students have identified the functions, have them exchange their article with another pair. Have them repeat the exercise and then compare versions and findings.

Teaching Advice: Working with Quotations

Quoting is ordinarily taught as a way to let the quoted person "speak for herself." But to what degree is that actually possible? Consider sharing with your students the perspective of Kay Halasek, who, in *A Pedagogy of Possibility*, builds on the work of Bakhtin and Volosinov to question traditional ways of teaching quoting as if this practice were ideologically or politically neutral. When we quote, after all, we take another's words out of context, putting them into contiguous relationship with our own words.

In addition, when we teach use of quotations as a way to build authority, we implicitly teach students to defer to the authority's quoted words. Halasek wisely suggests that we alert our students to these often invisible aspects of quoting and to show them at least some of the ways in which quotations can be used not to defer to an authority but to resist or even parody that "authority."

To check that students understand why they are using specific quotes, have them follow each excerpt in their text with an explanation of its significance.

Teaching Advice: Summarizing

Like the paraphrase, the summary is a useful learning and communicating skill. Writing summaries gives students practice identifying and coordinating the main points of a passage. Students don't have to write summaries using their own words, but if they rephrase the main points of an original passage, they will better understand what they are reading. This practice of rephrasing summarized (and paraphrased) information will also help them work source material into their research projects more easily. For this reason, discourage your students from simply pulling out phrases, sentences, or chunks of the original and then merely stringing them together.

Activity: Working with Quotations, Paraphrases, and Summaries

Ask students to bring in the rough draft of five pages of a research essay in progress, making sure to choose pages that include quotations, paraphrases, and summaries, and with all signal verbs and phrases underlined or highlighted. Then ask them to work in pairs to examine their use of these verbs and phrases. Can they explain why each signal verb or phrase was chosen and what rhetorical effect it has?

Teaching Advice: Checking for Excessive Use of Source Material

Recall the conversation analogy introduced at the beginning of this section. Have students review their drafts and ask themselves: "Am I still the moderator of this conversation? Is my voice clear, compelling, and original? Do I allow my own argument to emerge as foremost in this piece?" (Note that this last question may be difficult for multilingual writers familiar with different kinds of writing conventions. They may feel that emphasizing their own voice is rude or arrogant, or they may feel that they do not have the authority to advance their views.) Challenge them to see the emphasis of their own argument as a strategy of ethos, one of the most effective ways for persuading an audience. Indeed, writing instruction aims to build confidence and thereby to develop a compelling and informed voice that can contribute in important ways to the public sphere. As Bill Beattie observes: "The aim of education should be to teach us rather how to think, than what to think—rather to improve our minds, so as to enable us to think for ourselves, than to load the memory with thoughts of other men."

Have students use three different-colored highlighters: one for the signal phrase or verb, one for the quote itself, and one for the explanation of the quote. Students should be able to scan their paper to determine if they have an abundance of quotes in relation to their own writing.

Activity: Integrating Sources

To facilitate students' understanding of source integration, have them work in pairs to review each others' research essays. Ask them to analyze their partner's integration of sources, identifying any areas where source integration could be improved and considering visual as well as print sources. Have students write comments for each other and then spend time discussing their feedback in class.

Acknowledging Sources and Avoiding Plagiarism: Overview

A mark of intellectual maturity is the recognition of our debt to those whose ideas and insights have fostered the development of our own thinking and whose published and spoken texts have shaped our writing. Encourage your students to think of themselves as part of a larger community of scholars. Have them research the biographies and Web sites of authors whose books they cite; ask them to conceptualize their sources as people whose final texts began as ideas in writing classes and only developed into final form through years of writing, revision, and hard work. Often, when students reconsider sources as the work of writers and researchers who have toiled and struggled as they have, they are more likely to acknowledge sources for the information they glean from them. Ask students to identify each participant by name as he or she enters the text and the conversation unfolds.

Rebecca Moore Howard, director of the writing program at Syracuse University, challenges us as teachers to rethink our pedagogical approach to teaching proper use of sources:

> In our stampede to fight what *The New York Times* calls a "plague" of plagiarism, we risk becoming the enemies rather than the mentors of our students; we are replacing the student-teacher relationship with the criminal-police relationship. Further, by thinking of plagiarism as a unitary act rather than a collection of disparate activities, we risk categorizing all of our students as criminals. Worst of all, we risk not recognizing that our own pedagogy needs reform. (par. 7 from "Forget about Policing Plagiarism. Just *Teach*," published in the *Chronicle of Higher Education*)

Her insights are valuable ones; students often don't understand the nuances and complexities of proper citation. As Howard explains, "Encouraged by digital dualisms, we forget that plagiarism means many different things: downloading a term paper, failing to give proper credit to the source of an idea, copying extensive passages without attribution, inserting someone else's phrases or sentences—perhaps with small changes—into your own prose, and forgetting to supply a set of quotation marks" ("Forget" par. 11). Howard suggests that instead of relying on Web sites such as Turnitin.com or Plagiarism.org, we should develop more interesting and challenging assignments, foster increased dialogue on student drafts, and offer ourselves as an authentically engaged audience for student writing.

Nick Carbone provides a lengthy and insightful discussion of pedagogical approaches to possible plagiarism in his online column, "Technology and Teaching," on the Bedford/St. Martin's TechNotes Web site:

> Turnitin.com was originally founded by John Barrie—a neurobiology graduate student—as Plagiarism.org, which still exists as a marketing arm of Turnitin.com.
> . . . It assumes the worst about students and the worst about teachers. It assumes students have no honor and need always to be watched and followed electronically, a big brother welcome to academic traditions. It assumes teachers are too beleaguered and inept to design classroom assignments and practices that teach students how to write responsibly. Much of what Turnitin .com proposes to detect can be avoided by careful assignment planning and teaching . . . , by paying better attention early on to students and the work they do. (pars. 5 and 15)

Teaching Advice: Understanding Reasons to Acknowledge Sources

Take time to provide your students with a bit of historical perspective on acknowledging sources and plagiarism. You might explain the etymology of *plagiarism* and the way in which the demand for originality in writing impelled an ideology of ownership. As Peter Morgan and Glenn Reynolds tell us, it was not until the romantic era that the creation of new material became culturally paramount. In classical times, imitation was not a crime:

> The term "plagiarism" came from the word *plagiarius*, which literally meant "kidnapper." It was first used by the poet Martial regarding someone who had "kidnapped" some of his poems by copying them whole and circulating them under the copier's name. But while copying so as to take credit for another's work was wrong, use of another's work to create something of one's own was not. The goal was to take an idea that someone else might have had first, but to improve on it, or its execution. (par. 13 from "A Plague of Originality," published in *Idler*)

Help your students see the proper acknowledgment of sources as a professional, economic, and scholarly responsibility—one that respects the livelihoods of other writers—so that they can begin to understand why they need to be vigilant and extremely careful in their note-taking and writing processes. The following activity should aid you in doing this.

Activity: Knowing Which Sources to Acknowledge

Have students work in peer-review groups to review each other's drafts for any passages that stand out as unfamiliar and mark them with the highlighter. Often students can help point out to their peers what knowledge is most probably not readily available to them without the help of sources. Peer reviewers can also point out material that is "common knowledge" and doesn't need to be cited.

Teaching Advice: Maintaining Academic Integrity and Avoiding Plagiarism

As you prepare to discuss with students the important topic of academic integrity and plagiarism, consider for a moment how you will approach the subject and present it to your students.

In a lecture called "Why Is Plagiarism Wrong?" given at DePauw University on November 11, 1987, Barry M. Kroll outlined the five different approaches instructors take to discourage plagiarism. The most traditional—and apparently least effective—approach involves *prohibitions*. The instructor simply tells students, typically in moralistic terms, that plagiarism is wrong. Kroll warns us, "Virtually all college students already 'know' that plagiarism is a prohibited act. But despite that knowledge, a significant number of students do not appear to take the prohibition seriously enough to be dissuaded from plagiarizing in their college papers."

The second approach involves *prevention*, an attempt to make it difficult to plagiarize. Some strategies of this approach include assigning different textbooks and paper topics from term to term and not using books for which *Cliffs Notes* exist. Unfortunately, this approach does little to teach students not to plagiarize.

Some instructors and institutions try to deter students from plagiarizing by establishing *penalties* for those caught plagiarizing. This approach gains effectiveness when supported by the institution. However, it turns instructors into police, and most instructors dislike such a role. Such a role tends to undermine instructor-student rapport. More recent software, such as that available at Turnitin.com, similarly constructs a policing role for the writing instructor and breaks down the trust necessary for learning. It's much more effective to discuss the rationale for acknowledging sources, give students the benefit of the doubt, and provide excellent models for them to examine.

However, some instructors and institutions reject the notion that without penalties cheating would increase. Their remedy for plagiarism is to provide students with *practice* in using source material. This perspective assumes that most plagiarism is caused by unfamiliarity with the conventions of citation, sloppiness and neglect, and insufficient practice in citing sources. Unfortunately, we have ample evidence that students often do plagiarize intentionally.

The fifth approach to plagiarism—and the one that Kroll recommends—consists of teaching the *principles* behind society's attitudes toward plagiarism. In a separate study of how first-year students actually view plagiarism, Kroll discovered that they understood what it was and took it seriously, and that they could explain the wrongness of plagiarism with reference to three principles: fairness to authors, responsibility to one's education, and ownership of ideas. The latter two principles, Kroll argues, are inadequate, and the first incomplete. Kroll found no reference by students to the idea that plagiarism is wrong because it is deception. Yet Kroll recommends that principle as being the best argument against plagiarism. Such deception is morally unacceptable and is detrimental to the institution, to the community, and to the character of the individual. Moreover, this principle is the basis for the other approaches: "For unless our students understand the reasons that plagiarism is wrong and destructive, they are likely to see our prohibitions as outmoded, to see the practices of careful documentation as merely tedious exercises, and to see the penalties for plagiarism as irrationally punitive." In the final analysis, plagiarism can be both personally and rhetorically devastating. Whatever the personal consequences, plagiarism inevitably undermines the writer's ethos. The writer who plagiarizes loses all authority, and thus persuasion becomes an impossibility.

In "Plagiarisms, Authorship, and the Academic Death Penalty," Rebecca Moore Howard raises a number of additional issues that, as instructors of writing, we should consider, such as examining our own assumptions and preconceptions about the ownership of texts and ideas as preparation for discussing these issues with students. After discussing plagiarism, you might assign students the following activity, which should help them become clearer about their own thoughts on the topic.

Activity: Considering Your Intellectual Property

Have students work in groups of two or three to investigate their own definitions of intellectual property and plagiarism. The group members should take notes on how they arrived at the definitions and on their points of agreement and disagreement. Review these notes in a closing class discussion.

Writing a Research Project: Overview

The contemporary idea of "research" for an essay seems not to have gained much currency in college classrooms until the older idea of all reading (and especially the keeping of commonplace books) as research began to fade during the nineteenth century. Robert Connors notes that as students could be "counted on less and less for the sorts of commonplace knowledge that the older classical curriculum specialized in, teachers found general assignments worked less and less well. One solution was to ask students to go to the library (a place not easily accessible for most people, even college students, until about 1869 and after) and look up information in books." But this solution only led to more difficulties, notably copying verbatim or "plagiarizing." As a result, according to Connors, "teachers came to turn more and more to assignments that had at least some element of first-person experience." Research could then be used to support this experience, and such assignments grew increasingly common during the 1890s. The first handbook to include a full chapter on the research paper appears to have been Hodges's 1941 *Harbrace Handbook*, and by the 1950s this assignment was firmly entrenched in the college curriculum.

The idea of writing a research-based essay for class may seem daunting to many students, especially first-year composition students or students who have never written more than a brief response paper. Your job will be as much to motivate, inspire, and lead them through this process as it will be to supervise their research and writing. Most of all, students need encouragement and assurance that they can indeed join the community of scholars.

Teaching Advice: Refining Your Plans

Before students start to write, they should consider the following questions:

- What is your central purpose? What other purposes, if any, do you have?
- What is your stance toward your topic? Are you an advocate, a critic, a reporter, an observer?
- What audience(s) are you addressing?
- How much background information does your audience need?
- What supporting information will your readers find convincing— examples? quotations from authorities? statistics? graphs, charts, or other visuals? data from your own observations or from interviews?
- Should your tone be that of a colleague, an expert, a student?

- How can you establish common ground with your readers and show them that you have considered points of view other than your own?
- What is your working thesis trying to establish? Will your audience accept it?

To help your students appreciate the value of these questions, point out that they help students

1. Identify the intended audience.
2. Judge whether to define basic terms or to take for granted that the audience is already familiar with the research topic. For example, students wouldn't need to define *regeneration* for an audience of senior-level students working in molecular genetics or *apartheid* for senior-level political science students. But in a paper examining *economic disparity* in South Africa that they are writing for a composition class, they might want to define and explain that term fully.
3. Evaluate their sources and determine how to use them. For a general audience, students cannot assume that a simple mention of a researcher's claims will give the audience sufficient understanding. If the source material requires an advanced level of understanding, careful explanations will be necessary.
4. Consider how to present themselves to the audience, how to define their relationship with the audience, and how to establish common ground with audience members.
5. Consider further how they view their subject. What are they trying to prove or explain? What is their purpose in relation to the audience?
6. Reconsider the thesis with a specific audience in mind. Is the thesis unfamiliar to the audience? Or is it a reexamination of something the audience already assumes or accepts?

Activity: Working on a Thesis Statement

Call on one student to present his or her thesis to the class. Ask the writer to clarify or define any unfamiliar terms or vague points. Also ask the student to explain his or her topic choice. Then open up the class to a brainstorming session in which the student writer elaborates on the thesis and purpose by answering the questions posed by members of the class. In fielding the class's questions, the writer will clarify the project in his or her own mind, noting where difficulties lie, where command of the subject is lacking, and where elaboration is warranted. The writer may also discover that the topic is too broad and that the thesis needs some refining.

Once you have demonstrated this activity for the whole class, have students work in groups of two or three to develop each other's thesis statements.

Teaching Advice: Organizing Information

Just as we all have different preferred modalities for learning, we also have different approaches to organizing information. Engage your students in discussion about how they shape their research notes into a draft. Do they begin with an outline? Do they freewrite several pages to discover their direction? Do they group information by subject headings? Then you can help students get clearer about organization by assigning the "Organizing Information" activity on this page.

Outlining

The point cannot be overemphasized: a full formal outline is devilishly hard to write before one has actually produced at least a revised draft. A working outline is all that students should expect to produce. It can tentatively guide or reflect their planning. Assure your students that an outline is flexible. It mainly serves as a rough plan that enables them to start writing and organizing information. It is subject to revision once they've started writing. This advice rests on the thinking that not until writers put something down on paper can they really judge and plan the appropriateness of the content and format to purpose and audience. Help students develop their outlining skills by engaging them in the activity "Outlining" below.

Activity: Organizing Information

A new program at Stanford University called "How I Write: Conversations with Faculty" allows students to hear firsthand about the research strategies of senior faculty members across the disciplines. By learning about different strategies for approaching research and producing texts, students become critically aware of their own writing processes. One student, Angela, reflected, "I was glad to find that I wasn't the only one who gets stuck when I write . . . other students and even other professors do, too! I guess it is always a challenge to write something that really expresses what you want to say, and that's why it always takes a longer time to revise and revise, until you are satisfied with the writing."

Set up a similar conversation in your own classroom by asking students to interview each other about the writing process. How do they approach the organization of information? Do they need music or food in order to write? How do they work through writer's block? Do they rely on an outline or note cards grouped by subject headings?

Activity: Outlining

Ask students to exchange drafts of their research projects and outline their drafts using the text alone—that is, without asking for clarification from the writer. Next, have each pair examine these outlines together. How well does the outline reflect what the student writer intended in the draft? What points, if any, are left out? What does the outline suggest about the organization of the draft and the coverage of the topic? In what ways can the outline help the student revise the draft?

Teaching Advice: Drafting

Almost all students now compose on computers. With their cut-and-paste function, quick saving capability, and interface with online databases and image banks, computers are effective for drafting research-based essays. However, there are several practical tips for working with technology that you should bring to the attention of your students:

- *Save often*—and not just on the hard drive. You might ask students to use a thumb drive to back up their work. Students can send backup copies to their email accounts or upload copies to file storage sites such as Google Docs.

- *Print out draft versions.* Encourage students to print out their drafts at each stage in order to keep a record of their writing process. A printed copy can also be a lifesaver if the document file is lost.

- *Revise on paper as well as onscreen.* Remind students that revising and editing an entire paper document versus blocks of text on a screen can differ in significant ways. Ask them to reflect on the kinds of revisions they tend to make on paper versus on a computer screen.

Activity: Introductions and Conclusions

Have students work in groups of five to brainstorm lists of specific purposes for the introduction and the conclusion. Once they've compiled these lists, ask them to find articles in major journals in various fields and to note the writers' purposes in several introductions and conclusions. Here are some possibilities they may come up with:

1. *Introductions*
   State the problem or topic to be explored.
   Give briefly the background or context for the question or topic.
   Get readers interested.
   Give briefly the reason for discussing or researching a topic.

2. *Conclusions*
   Answer the question initially raised in the introduction.
   Confirm the hypothesis.
   Repeat the main idea or point that the article has worked to explain.
   Confirm the importance of the question or subject.
   Suggest areas for further research.

Resources

Section	The St. Martin's Handbook	The Everyday Writer	EasyWriter
Considering the Research Process	10a	14	38a
Analyzing the Assignment	10b	14a	38a
Narrowing a Topic	10c	7a	38a
Moving from Research Question to Hypothesis	10d	14b	38a
Making a Preliminary Research Plan	10f	14c	38a
Keeping a Research Log	10g	14d	38a
Moving from Hypothesis to Working Thesis	10h	14e	38a
Differentiating Kinds of Sources	11a	15a	38b
Using the Library to Get Started	11b	15b	38c
Finding Library Resources	11c	15c	38c
Conducting Internet Research	11d	15d	38d
Conducting Field Research	11e	15e	38e
Using Sources to Meet a Need	12a	16a	
Keeping a Working Bibliography	12b	16b	
Evaluating Usefulness and Credibility	12c	16c	39a
Reading and Interpreting Sources	12d	16d	39b
Synthesizing Sources	12e	16e	39c
Taking Notes and Annotating Sources	12f	16f	39d

Deciding Whether to Quote, Paraphrase, or Summarize	13a	17a	40a
Working with Quotations	13b	17b	40a
Summarizing	13d	17b	40a
Checking for Excessive Use of Source Material	13f	17d	40a
Understanding Reasons to Acknowledge Sources	14a	17e	40c
Knowing Which Sources to Acknowledge	14b	17f	40c
Maintaining Academic Integrity and Avoiding Plagiarism	14c	17g	40d
Refining Your Plans	15a	18a	41
Organizing Information	15b	18b	41
Drafting	15c	18b	41a

Note: Depending on which book you are using, student essays may appear online rather than in print. Check the Directory of Student Writing for locations.

Peer Review and Revision

Reviewing and Revising: Overview

> *"I never have time to rewrite; I always wait until the night before."*
> *"How can I improve my first draft when I don't know whether it's good?"*
> *"I don't care about what I'm writing. I just want to get it over with."*
> *"I'm such a bad writer that I hate to read my own writing."*
> *"If I can't get it right the first time, I must be stupid."*

Such typical attitudes toward revision support Erika Lindemann's claim that "for most students, rewriting is a dirty word." Students tend to view rewriting as an indication of failure, as punishment, or as simply a "filler" for classroom time. Because students have often been trained to outline carefully or to follow the format of a five-paragraph essay, revising means nothing more than making their words "prettier" or moving from handwriting to type or fixing misspelled words and mispunctuated sentences. In fact, many student writers are under the misapprehension that "real" writing is perfectly formed and flows onto the page at the touch of the Muse's hand. It is important for them to realize that almost all experienced writers revise their work repeatedly.

Marcel Proust wrote that "the real voyage of discovery consists not in seeking new landscapes, but in having new eyes." Revision *is* a process of "*re*-vision" or looking at an essay with new eyes. You can help students grasp the benefits of rigorous review and in-depth revision by sharing with them Proust's insight and teaching them to look at rewriting as a journey of discovery.

Teaching Advice: Rereading Your Draft

When instructing students to reread their drafts, be sure to distinguish between revising and editing. Students often confuse revising (making changes in content) with editing (correcting mechanical errors). To reinforce this important distinction:

1. Try to observe the distinction yourself.
2. Discuss revising and editing on separate days, as separate class topics.
3. Plan separate practice exercises for revising and editing.

Finally, try to structure your assignment schedules with ample time for students to be able to look at a piece of writing with fresh eyes. In particular, check to see that there is sufficient space between the due dates for the rough draft, the peer review, and the final version. The following activity should also help students strengthen their rereading skills.

Activity: Rereading Your Draft

Have students post their papers online through an electronic discussion board or a course Web site. Provide students with an online peer-review sheet, asking them questions based on the information in this section. (See the cross-reference chart on page 137.) Ask students to assess their own draft through the lens of these questions. You can then move into peer review; but it is crucial to develop in students the ability to reread their drafts from a more impartial and critical vantage point. Vary this exercise by having students read one another's drafts focusing on just one area: meaning, purpose, audience, stance, organization, or use of visuals.

Teaching Advice: Reviewing Peer Writers

Having students respond to each other's work is probably the most common type of collaboration in composition classes. Peer review helps students (1) move beyond an exclusive focus on the instructor as audience; (2) learn to accept and use constructive criticism; (3) practice analyzing written texts, including their own; and (4) acquire the vocabulary of composition.

Nevertheless, many students are reluctant to share their writing with other students. They may regard the instructor as the only one qualified to give advice or criticism; hence, time spent with peers is perceived as wasted time. Moreover, some students are embarrassed to show what they fear is poor writing to peers who will judge them personally. They lack experience in offering constructive criticism. Your students may need help in learning how to respond to one another's work—how to temper excessive criticism with tact, how to balance *what* has been said with *how* it has been said, both in terms of the writer's text and the reader's comments. In this way they will learn how to respond to drafts and how to trust and help one another, both vital aspects of a productive composition course.

To make sure your students are offering more than yes/no comments when reviewing other writers' drafts, consider collecting and evaluating their responses. Reinforce specific responses that quote a word or phrase or that refer to a specific paragraph or line. Your interest will underscore the value of peer response.

Having worked in groups, your students could have as many as four or five sets of responses to their writing. Lest they be overwhelmed by so many suggestions and questions, assure them that they need not heed all the advice, just weigh it. However, if several comments point in the same direction, the writer should take them seriously.

When students are faced with conflicting advice, they will naturally turn to you for the "right" answer. Because this is an impossible request, you will have to encourage them to reach their own decisions. Have them ask other students to respond to their particular problems. Ask about their original writing choices and about the potential effect of suggested changes. Using others' comments to make independent decisions should be a goal of every writer.

Ideally, peer-review sessions will be so effective, profitable, and stimulating that your students will initiate sessions outside the classroom. Realistically, however, they will probably hesitate to ask others who have no peer-review experience or training. Therefore, you may want to provide them with several questions or statements for introducing a session:

1. "Would you mind telling me what you think of this?"
2. "The point I want to make in this paper is _____."
3. "How well did I succeed?"
4. "What do you think of my support?"
5. "I had trouble with this part. Does it make sense to you? What can I do to improve it?"

At least once during the term, have students initiate a review session with someone other than a classmate. Ask them to report on their success. The following two activities offer some ways to put this advice into action.

Activity: Reviewing Peer Writers 1

Have students compose online entries or threaded email responses on their perceptions of the advantages and disadvantages of peer review. Have them respond to each other's entries or put together a class Web page on the possibilities and potential problems. Knowing their concerns will allow you to explain the nature of peer review more fully and thus alleviate many of their initial concerns. Having them communicate their concerns will help build class community and alleviate individual fears. Then you can more easily model and introduce collaborative writing activities (including the ones in this chapter).

Activity: Reviewing Peer Writers 2

Here are a few exercises you can use to help students gain comfort sharing their drafts and learning to give and receive critiques:

1. At the beginning of the term, have groups of students read and comment on one another's writing. You may wish to suggest a number of your own questions as well as those in the text to help them respond to what they read: What is most memorable or stands out most in what they are reading? What is the writer's main point—and what makes that point clear or not clear? How does the essay in question respond to the assignment?
2. Using an anonymous, imperfect model draft, provide at least one or two practice sessions before the class undertakes its first peer-review session. During these preliminary discussions, check their responses and help students who have trouble offering comments.
3. To encourage group discussion, you may wish to share one of your own preliminary drafts or an example of a work in progress and have students comment on it.

4. Ask your students to keep a record of peer responses to their work. Do certain problems recur? As they become increasingly aware of their writing profiles, your students will develop self-critical faculties that they can apply to their own writing. What they can do today in group discussion with peers, they will be able to do individually and by themselves in the future.

5. Group students into threes or fours and have each student read her or his paper aloud to the others. The students then vote on which of the papers they think is the strongest; make sure they can articulate why. Then pair the groups, so that the larger group has two strong papers. Again, have those students read their papers aloud to the group, and have the group vote on the strongest of the two papers. Encourage discussion to articulate why one paper is stronger than the other. Finally, have the students with the resulting strong papers (likely three to four at this point, depending on the size of the class) read them aloud to the whole class, and have the students discuss which one is the strongest and why.

Teaching Advice: Learning from Instructor Comments

One of the most frustrating and troubling experiences for a student in college can be when the student can neither read nor understand the comments provided on an essay. To avoid this, take time at the beginning of class to review your expectations for submitted work. Distribute a brief handout explaining the kinds of marginal and closing comments you are likely to provide on student writing. You might even create a chart, showing the shorthand words and symbols you will use and what they mean. Alternatively, you could give students a copy of a commented paper from a previous class (with the student writer's permission, of course) to illustrate and review your process of providing feedback. Most important, however, you should take time to explain your reasons for making the kinds of comments you anticipate making and to illustrate to students how you hope your feedback will enable them to improve and develop as writers at the college level. Then, use the following activities.

Purpose

When designing your writing assignments, list "Purpose" as a separate category in order to develop students' critical thinking about the importance of purpose in the writing process. Ask students to compare the purposes of writing done for different classes and different audiences. Have students bring in the prompts for writing assignments distributed in other classes and participate in a group analysis of the language of these documents. A class dialogue on purpose, using concrete examples from students' courses and extracurricular activities, will help illuminate this concept.

Paragraph Structure

You can use post-draft outlines to emphasize the importance of logical paragraph structure in the writing process. Ask students to make an outline of the points covered in their drafts, and then have them assess the effectiveness of their paragraph order and structure. You might give students a list of questions to answer, including the following:

- Do the paragraphs help readers follow the thread of thought?
- Is there a tendency to use underdeveloped paragraphs (one or two sentences in length)?
- Does each paragraph deal with one significant idea (or are there too many)?
- Is there a cumulative development of ideas from beginning to end?
- Does the argument build or do the paragraphs need to be rearranged/restructured to provide a more forceful progression?
- Are there strong transitions between paragraphs?

Documentation

Students respond well to checklists that help them assess proper documentation. You can provide the following questions to help them work on their drafts in peer-review groups before turning in a final revision:

- Are there specific primary sources cited throughout the essay?
- Are there secondary sources integrated as frame and support for the argument?
- Is all the material in the quotes necessary and appropriate?
- Are quotes integrated well (with proper signal phrases), so that the context or source is understood?
- Is there sufficient analysis and explanation after each quotation to propel the argument forward?

For MLA Citation

- Is there a source reference for every quotation?
- Are page numbers or paragraph numbers cited parenthetically after each quotation?
- Does each citation list the author's last name (or, if no author, the title's key words)?
- Are quotes of four lines or more introduced with a colon and indented five spaces?
- Are quotes of less than four lines set off with quotation marks?
- Does the format follow MLA style with punctuation after the parenthesis?
- Is the works-cited list in correct MLA format?

In addition to distributing checklists to students, it is worth spending time in class discussing the importance of proper documentation. Analogies to scientific notation (for science majors), correct "code" (for computer science majors), or proper form and training (for athletes) often work to open students' minds to considering the value of proper format.

Activity: Revising with Peer and Instructor Comments 1

Ask students to bring in copies of papers they have received back from instructors in other classes. Have them make a chart of the kinds of feedback they were given. The students can work in small groups, aiding each other in translating the comments into lessons about how to improve as writers and thinkers.

Each group should then compose a short "message pitch": What is the message the writer is being given through the comments? How can all students in class learn from these comments several strategies for developing and growing as college writers?

Activity: Revising with Peer and Instructor Comments 2

Ask students to find a recent essay or assignment with instructor comments on organizational issues and to bring the example to class for discussion. Ask students to write a short letter to that instructor. Their letters should do three things:

1. Respond to the instructor's comments, telling that instructor what they think he or she is asking them to do.
2. Explain why the students organized their writing in the way they did in the first place.
3. Explain how they would reorganize the essay or assignment according to the instructor's comments and their own improved understanding.

Activity: Revising with Peer and Instructor Comments 3

Using a computer projector, display sample writing passages from student papers to demonstrate the effective use of sources. A large computer screen or shared plasma screen works particularly well, as all students can see the text on the screen.

Once you display a sample text, ask students to participate in analyzing the use of the source as evidence: Is there an effective lead-in to the citation? Does the passage identify the source of the citation? Is there an effective comment on the citation to propel the argument forward? Solicit suggestions for revision from the students, and make changes with the keyboard, demonstrating each correction to the class.

Try to offer different kinds of examples when teaching the proper use of sources. For instance, demonstrate a paraphrase, summary, and direct quotation. Show students how to integrate visual sources into their writing. Provide a Web source, an e-text of a published article, and a book entry. Use this opportunity to begin a conversation about the evaluation of sources and the importance of consulting a range of sources.

Teaching Advice: Revising Thesis and Support

Ask students to bring their drafts to class for analysis. Have them circle or highlight the thesis statements on their drafts. Then ask them to check paragraph by paragraph to make sure each one relates back to the thesis and offers support for the main argument of the essay. Where there are discrepancies, students should strengthen the topic sentence of a paragraph or revise the thesis to accommodate the idea.

Activity: Rethinking Organization 1

Ask your students to locate a story, an article, or a book they especially enjoyed reading. Either in class or as homework, have them analyze the piece by outlining its organization. Then ask them to answer the following questions and cite examples from the text:

1. Why do you suppose the author started this way? Is there a flashback? a provocative question? a description?
2. Does the author "hook" you? If so, how?
3. At what point in the piece did you become interested and decide to go on?
4. How is the piece held together? Find appropriate transitional devices, repetition of key words, or repetitive sentence structures.
5. How does the author prepare you for the information in the middle and the end of the piece?
6. How does the author end the piece? Was it satisfying to you? predictable? surprising?

In class, discuss students' responses to the questions. How can they apply their responses to their own written drafts?

Activity: Rethinking Organization 2

Assign each student a partner; ask students to read and outline each other's essays. This activity will give students an idea of how well their organization comes across. If possible, and if time allows, have students exchange essays with more than one reviewer so they can compare various outlines of their essays. This exchange will help all students pinpoint possible areas of confusion.

A useful kind of outlining exercise is the "Says/Does" outline: have students examine each paragraph in terms of what it "says" (the point of the paragraph) and what it "does" (how the paragraph functions in the essay as a whole and/or in relationship to preceding and subsequent paragraphs). Students can write their "says/does" responses in the margins.

Activity: Revising Titles 1

With students working in groups of three, have them review each other's drafts and answer the following questions:

- Look at the title. Does it seem appropriate to you now that you've finished the piece? Why, or why not?
- Did the title seem appropriate when you started reading?
- Can you improve on the title or provide an alternative?

Activity: Revising Titles 2

A great way to get students to understand the importance of titles is through an assessment of their function. Begin by discussing the crucial aspects of titles—what function they serve and what makes them effective. Students might suggest the following attributes that you can write on the board or project from a computer screen (we call this list the "three *I*s for effective titles"):

- informative (or clear and relevant to the topic)
- interesting (or captivating—perhaps through humor, shock, or emotion)
- indicates stance (or begins to suggest the writer's thesis or perspective on the topic)

Once you have discussed this working rubric, ask students to evaluate each other's titles. This activity works well in a computer-networked classroom, where you can cut and paste the titles of all students' drafts into a PowerPoint presentation while they are in peer-review groups. Then lead them through a slide show in which you show increasing levels of complexity, from simple one-word titles to more engaging, funny, and elaborate titles. Make the presentation interactive by asking students for on-the-spot revisions as you go. At the end of class, ask them to read out loud their revised titles and save them for future use. (Note: If you can't create a PowerPoint presentation during peer review in class, then simply ask students to post or email their papers to you so you can develop the presentation before your class meeting.)

Activity: Revising Introductions

"First impressions count," Emily Post wrote, speaking about one's manners and personal appearance. Similarly, the writer's introductory paragraph gives the reader a first impression of the writer. Have students work in small groups to answer the following questions about the effectiveness of their introductory paragraphs:

1. What tentative conclusions can you draw about the writer's style and tone from the introduction? Is the writer intelligent, well-informed, and confident? Is the writer ill at ease or uncommitted to the topic?
2. Can you determine the intended audience from the first paragraph? Or does the introduction seem to be directed at no one in particular? Describe the intended audience.

Activity: Revising Conclusions

Padded endings are common in student writing. Inexperienced writers may sense that the paper is finished, but lacking confidence in their own writing, may feel compelled to restate the thesis or summarize the entire essay. Have students find and copy into their logs the endings (the final paragraph or sentence) of three to five essays or articles they particularly like. Have them each select an ending to share in class and discuss the features that make it effective. Then have them read the endings of their own essays aloud in small groups to see if they can identify any possibilities for making them more effective (more concise, clear, powerful, and so on).

Teaching Advice: Revising Paragraphs, Sentences, Words, and Tone

Students often think that becoming a better writer means that one does not have to attend to the smaller units of composition—paragraphs, sentences, words, and tone. But even the most prolific and accomplished writers struggle with revision of these small parcels of meaning. The popular humor writer Dave Barry offers the following reflection on revision, which you might want to share with your students:

> Writing humor takes discipline and hard work. I have this theory. Here it is, My Theory about Writing: It's hard. The humor doesn't just flow as easily as people think. A funny idea has to be tooled and shaped so that it's funny to others when it's read. People think that because humor is light and easy to read that it's just as simple to write. Nothing could be more untrue. You have to work at it. Writer's block, for example. Here's My Theory about Writer's Block: People simply give up and don't want to put forth the effort to work through the barriers. No good writing is easy. It has to do with overcoming the obstacles we find in the way of our creativity. You have to have the determination to do it.   —Dave Barry, *How to Write Funny*

The following advice and activities should help you teach students how to work on revising different smaller units of composition.

Revising Words

Joseph Williams, in *Style: Ten Lessons in Clarity and Grace*, points out that avoiding passives and agentless constructions will usually make one's choice of words more vigorous and direct. He gives these examples for comparison:

> The money was found by me.

> I found the money.

However, as Williams points out, "often we don't say who is responsible for an action, because we don't know or don't care, or because we'd just rather not say." Consider the following examples:

> The president *was rumored* to have considered resigning.

> Those who *are* guilty of negligence *can be fined.*

> Valuable records *should always be kept* in a fire-proof safe.

After giving students these examples, have them select one page of a current draft and highlight every passive construction they can locate. They can work individually, in pairs, or in groups to determine whether each instance of the passive voice is justified or not.

Revising Tone

Word choice produces tone, and tone carries implications for a writer's voice. The work of theorist Mikhail Bakhtin has been particularly useful in helping to examine traditional notions of voice as something unique and authentic to any individual. This view, much elaborated and advocated by Peter Elbow, Donald Murray, and many others in composition studies, fails to recognize the constructed nature of all voices. More important, it fails to recognize the multiplicity (what Bakhtin calls "heterogeneity") of voice. Like all writers, students have many voices they can deploy in various ways, and these voices are always, according to Bakhtin, in dialogue with others. Teachers can help students locate differing voices in their texts, some their "own" and others that belong to institutional discourse, such as the voice of big business or of higher education. Moreover, instructors can teach students how to study and learn from the tensions among these voices. By emphasizing that students examine carefully their use of words or diction, teachers can begin to raise student awareness about the presence and importance of voice in writing.

Activity: Revising Paragraphs 1

You can use post-draft outlines to emphasize the importance of logical paragraph structure in the writing process. Ask students to make an outline of the points covered in their drafts, and then have them assess the effectiveness of their paragraph order and structure. You might give students a list of questions to answer, including the following:

- Do the paragraphs help readers follow the thread of thought?
- Is there a tendency toward underdeveloped paragraphs (one or two sentences in length)?
- Does each paragraph deal with one significant idea—or too many?
- Is there a cumulative development of ideas from beginning to end?
- Does the argument build or do the paragraphs need to be rearranged/restructured to provide a more forceful progression?
- Are there strong transitions between paragraphs?

Activity: Revising Paragraphs 2

Assign a draft due at the start of class. Ask the students to identify the best three- to five-sentence paragraph from the draft. After dividing the class into small groups, ask each student to read his or her paragraph to the rest of the group. The rest of the group then decides which passage is most effective and analyzes it for sentence length, sentence variety, word choice, and tone. Accentuate the positive and encourage possible revisions.

Activity: Revising Paragraphs 3

Have students work in groups of three or four to compare and contrast the paragraph structures in a popular magazine (such as *Time* or *Newsweek*), academic journal (*Critical Inquiry* or the *Journal of Modern History*), or blog (*Slate* or the *Huffington Post*) of their choosing. Ask students to note that paragraph length, organization, layout, and use of visuals vary. Ask each group to write a short response essay on the following question: how do the paragraphs you looked at compare with those you and your classmates typically write?

Activity: Revising Sentences

Have students exchange papers in peer-review groups and use pens to circle repetitive phrases in their sentences. Often a particular pattern will emerge in student writing, and each student can develop an awareness of his or her own individual tendencies by having peers help identify these patterns. Students can use a highlighter to emphasize particularly compelling phrases in the work of their writing groups. Ask students to share their findings with each other and to discuss the benefits of different sentence lengths, sentence sequences, and ordering strategies.

Editing and Reflecting: Overview

It is often difficult to convince students how important critical reflection, revision, and editing are to the writing process. Often, they think that their first draft should be their final draft and that some minor changes suffice for editing. The advice and activities that follow will be useful in getting students to develop their editing skills—in general and with regard to specific, tricky problems like sentence openings and length—as well as their abilities to reflect seriously about their writing.

Activity: Editing

Even writing that has reached final draft stage can be revised through one last editing pass, and often very effectively. Have students choose two paragraphs from Emily Lesk's final draft and, working with two or three other students, plan and carry out a last editing pass. They should begin by reading the paragraphs aloud once or twice and jotting down items in three columns: a "plus" column for words, phrases, or ideas they especially like; a "minus" column for words, phrases, or ideas they *don't* like; and a "question" column for words, phrases, or ideas that seem unclear or questionable. Then they can compare notes all around and, together, draft a revision plan to change words or phrases that were not as strong as they could be. Finally, have them compare their edits with the original paragraphs and report to the class, explaining the changes and describing what they have done to improve the essay as a whole through this final editing.

Activity: Sentence Openings

Have students underline the first four words of each sentence in several random paragraphs. If the basic syntax is the same in too many sentences, ask them to find ways to reword the sentence, by beginning with dependent clauses.

Teaching Advice: Sentence Length

Ask students to choose two random paragraphs from their paper and count the words in each sentence. If the number for each sentence is too similar, ask them to combine and condense their sentences for variety in length.

Activity: Opening with *It* and *There*

Following are two sentences featuring *it is* or *there is* from the first draft of a student's paper. Ask students to work collaboratively with a classmate to make at least two revisions that eliminate these constructions. All pairs of students should bring their revisions to class and be prepared to explain their revision process.

1. In today's world of CNN, e-journals, and Newsweek.com, it is often easy to forget how pervasive a medium the magazine was prior to the advent of television.

2. There is no denying that this strategy worked brilliantly, as this inviting image of Santa Claus graduated from the pages of *Saturday Evening Post* to become the central figure of the most celebrated and beloved season of the year.

After your students have written two versions of each of the *there is* and *it is* sentences, ask them to see how many variations they can create as a class.

Teaching Advice: Proofreading the Final Draft

Many students cut out the final stage of proofreading because they are eager to finish, because they stay up too late, or because they lose interest in the writing. You may want to provide them a last-minute opportunity to proofread and make final edits. Before they hand in their papers, give them ten minutes of class time to read over their final drafts; or ask them to trade papers and proofread one another's final drafts.

Teaching Advice: A Student's Revised Draft

Distribute an early and a late draft of a paper from a previous class and have students read both versions and discuss. Ask them to write a one-page summary of the specific ways the revised version differs from the original draft and explain why those differences strengthen or weaken the paper.

Teaching Advice: Portfolios

One of the best ways to capture the kinds of changes that take place over time with the writing process is by assembling either a print or electronic writing portfolio. One salutary result of the "process" movement in composition studies has been the increased understanding of how and when particular student writers move back and forth among the acts of inventing, revising, drafting, editing, rethinking, drafting, and so on, most often in nonlinear and highly recursive ways; portfolios are one way to document that process. In turn, these new understandings have highlighted the importance of critical thinking to writing, not only in terms of invention and expression of ideas, but also in more global ways.

Often referred to as *metadiscourse*, this high-order kind of critical thinking calls on writers to step back and survey their own work, analyzing its strengths and weaknesses and articulating its inner workings—its diction, syntax, and rhetoric. Research in composition indicates that the ability to exercise this kind of critical thinking is an important part of what enables growth in writing.

At the same time, the benefits to the student of assembling a writing portfolio are immeasurable. By tracking, compiling, and reflecting on their work, the way their writing has changed, and how they have developed strategies of invention, composition, and delivery, students produce a metadiscourse about the recursive nature of their writing lives. Moreover, once introduced to the value of assembling and maintaining a writing portfolio, students often continue the practice throughout their academic and professional careers. In this way, they continue to learn about themselves as writers and as critical thinkers.

The overlapping terms *portfolio, journal, log, diary,* and *daybook* refer to a wide range of writing practices whose origins may be as old as writing itself. Thus, when you lead students in the assembly and completion of portfolios, take time to explain how these various writing genres all serve a similar purpose: the portfolio is a crafted representation of the writer's work. However, as an instructor, you should be clear in your own mind what purpose you want the portfolio to serve: Do you want it to be a showcase portfolio—a collection of the best work from a specific course? Do you want it to be a process portfolio—a collection of work that documents progress through drafts, revisions, and final copies? Do you want it to function as a professional portfolio that students could use for job searches (common in art, teaching, and nursing disciplines)? Will the portfolio be used to evaluate or assess the student? the program? What portion of the course grade will it be? What criteria will you use to evaluate it?

When giving students guidance on what elements to include in their portfolios, be sure to spend time discussing the importance of organization and format. In *Visual Communication: A Writer's Guide,* Susan Hilligoss and Tharon Howard delineate some of the key concerns students should keep in mind when designing portfolios: a portfolio is a unique genre, with much opportunity for visual creativity, yet it calls for many of the navigational features of more conventional long documents. Because it projects the writer's ethos and because readers may be rushed or unfamiliar with portfolio layouts, the portfolio should have a unified look, a visual impact that supports the ethos and the communicative purpose, and clear organization.

As Richard Larson argues in "Portfolios in the Assessment of Writing," *portfolio* should designate "an ordered compilation of writings. A casual gathering up of papers one has written over a year or two probably does not deserve to be called a 'portfolio.' A portfolio ideally should be a deliberate compilation, gathered according to some plan, for use by an identified reader or readers for specific needs or purposes." Teachers who wish to use portfolios in their classrooms or programs might well begin by following Larson's lead here: determine the principles by which the portfolio will be compiled, decide how it will be organized, identify the intended audience(s) for the portfolio, and enumerate the purposes the portfolio will serve. You should emphasize to students the three key concepts of a portfolio: collect, select, and reflect.

The following activity should help students get a handle on these concepts.

Activity: Portfolios

If your entire class is built around a portfolio, then you will have determined the portfolio's purposes and the criteria by which it will be evaluated. However, if the portfolio is only a portion of your class or if it is an option, then, if possible, engage students in developing the criteria by which their portfolios will be evaluated. This way, the entire class participates in the portfolio planning process. Ask students to work in groups to come up with at least half a dozen (or more if possible) items they think are characteristic of first-rate portfolios. Use these lists as the basis for class discussion on how you can recognize these characteristics in the pieces of writing in the portfolio and how credit should be apportioned for them. Then if the portfolio is to be a major part of your course, you might wish to have students form groups of three to work together as an editorial board, reviewing and responding to one another's portfolios throughout the term.

Suggest that students work in groups of two or three to brainstorm what each of them would most like his or her portfolio to accomplish—and which pieces of writing will best meet these goals. Students should take notes during their conversations with team members and bring these notes to class for discussion. Each team member should be prepared to explain his or her choices for the portfolio.

Teaching Advice: Reflective Statements

Reflective statements can be structured in a variety of ways, but it is imperative that you clarify your expectations about what the statement should cover: Should it be comprehensive, including quotes from the papers as supporting statements, or should it focus on specific items determined by you or the students? Or do you want shorter reflective statements for specific assignments? For example, a reflective statement might be written as a letter to a reader other than the instructor; it might focus specifically on error analysis—explaining what specific errors have been identified and strengthened throughout the course; and it might also be an argumentative essay showing that the student has met the required outcomes for the class. Metacognitive writing takes practice, though, and you will want to teach the process and show models of the kind of writing you expect.

The self-reflection or assessment part of the writing process is as crucial to the development of critical thinking as are the reviewing, revising, and editing stages. To help students with the task of assessment, ask them to type a brief letter to their classmates and instructor addressing the following aspects:

- specific ways in which your writing has changed, developed, or improved
- understanding of rhetorical strategies and writing strategies
- ways in which you plan to apply insights and practices learned here to other contexts
- closing reflections on your participation in the class community during this term
- anything else you want to articulate concerning your work over the term

You might also ask students to refer specifically to at least three pieces of writing (or outlines, drafts, and revisions) that they have completed or to quote from their work to illustrate their points.

Resources

Section	The St. Martin's Handbook	The Everyday Writer	EasyWriter
Rereading Your Draft	4a	9a	2f–2g
Reviewing Peer Writers	4b	9b	2f–2g
Learning from Instructor Comments	4d	9c	2f–2g
Revising with Peer and Instructor Comments	4e	9c	2f–2g
Revising Thesis and Support	4f	9d	2f–2g
Rethinking Organization	4g	9d	2f–2g
Revising	4h–4i	9d	2f–2g
Editing	4k	10a	2h–2i
Proofreading the Final Draft	4l	10a	2h–2i
Portfolios and Reflective Statements	4m, 65	10b	2h–2i

Note: Depending on which book you are using, student essays may appear online rather than in print. Check the Directory of Student Writing for locations.

Multimodality

Thinking about Visuals and Media: Overview

No longer is a paper a self-sufficient entity. In the age of the Internet, students need to think about presentation more than ever—as well as about the way their writing relates to other media, especially visual media. The advice and activities in this chapter should help you engage students in thinking about these tough and important topics.

Teaching Advice: Visuals, Media, and Design

Sylvan Barnet and Hugo Bedau assert the necessity of assessing format and presentation in terms of visual persuasion. It may be helpful to share this rationale with your students: "Every paper uses some degree of visual persuasion, merely in its appearance: perhaps a title page, certainly margins (ample—but not so wide that they tell the reader that the writer is unable to write a paper of the assigned length), double spacing for the convenience of the reader, paragraphing (again for the convenience of the reader), and so on." Ask students to complete a format checklist in peer-review groups or on their own before handing in their revised drafts.

Often students overlook the importance of document design in their focus on content and purpose. Ask them to consider the impression that one makes in going to a job interview with the appropriate clothes and demeanor. Would someone wear crumpled, dirty, or inappropriate clothing? It's just as crucial for writers to attend to formal qualities of their writing, including overall organization, sentence structure and style, paragraph structure, format, documentation, and correct incorporation of visuals.

You can help facilitate such attention to the entire package and presentation of their work, from the opening words to the overall format of their essays, by providing students with a "final checklist" to use in assessing their last revisions. Give students a handout or post questions on your course Web site. Delineate your precise expectations for document design—or the way a paper will be formatted. It is also helpful to have a class dialogue about the different format expectations across disciplines and classes.

Teaching Advice: Thinking Critically about Visuals

The emphasis in composition classrooms on considering visual arguments is becoming more and more prominent in curricula across the country. From analyzing a photograph in the news to interrogating the function of a Web site, students are participating in the "pictorial turn" by moving from passive consumers to active readers and eventually writers of visual media. As Sylvan Barnet and Hugo Bedau remind us, "premises and assumptions tend to remain unstated in visual persuasion; deciphering them requires highly active reading." Whether visual images are found online or in a photo gallery, in a mall or on a monument, in combination with words or on their own, visual culture offers a form of argument that we need to consider in our writing classes.

Much theoretical work in visual culture has been done since W. J. T. Mitchell identified the "pictorial turn" in composition studies. New journals such as *Enculturation* merge visual cultural studies and rhetoric, while the Summer 2002 issue of *Kairos* (an online journal of rhetoric, technology, and pedagogy) hosts a series of articles exploring the intersections of technology, popular culture, and the art of teaching.

Teaching Advice: Working with Visuals

When teaching students to select and integrate visuals into their writing, be sure to discuss issues of copyright and permissions. Students should carefully note the source of the image. The use of visuals in students' papers is generally considered fair use, but like any source, visuals must be cited in the text. If students intend to post to an unprotected Web site any work that includes visuals from another source, they must seek permission from the rights holder.

Teaching Advice: Analyzing Visual Arguments

Doreen Piano, in "Analyzing a Web Zine," asks students to "choose a zine of interest to write a rhetorical and cultural analysis." As part of the assignment, students examine "not only textual aspects such as purpose, audience, design and layout, and content but [also] extra-linguistic features such as reception and consumption of the zine." Her purpose is to show students that the visual images help make the Internet "an ethnographic site, a space where people convene and create different kinds of cultures, some that are in opposition to mainstream culture or that present points of view that may not be represented in the media."

By emphasizing the point that visual arguments speak to an audience, you can help students apply their analysis of argument skills to visual images. Moreover, they can assess both content and design aspects with an eye to the larger purposes such visual arguments serve.

Activity: Analyzing Visual Arguments

Ask students to bring in examples of their favorite advertisements from print sources (such as magazines and campus or national newspapers) and the Internet. In small groups, have students use the following questions to examine the images:

- How does the design of the visual enhance or hinder the argument?
- What emotional appeals does the argument elicit, and how?

- What ethical appeals making the visual argument credible? Does it call on any authorities or symbols to establish character or credibility?

- How does the visual argument make logical appeals? Do words and images work together to create a logical cause-effect relationship? How are any examples used?

- What claim(s) does the visual argument make?

- What reasons are attached to the claim, and how well are they supported by evidence?

- What assumption(s) underlie the claim and the reasons?

Also have students ask what difference the medium makes (print versus digital; national press versus campus paper; fashion magazine versus independent journal).

Have each group select two images that work particularly well as visual arguments and present their analysis collaboratively to the class. Then, as a means of reinforcing what was learned, assign students the task of finding another, more subtle visual argument to bring to the next class.

Teaching Advice: Thinking about Genre

After reading and talking about this section, ask students to work in groups to compile three lists: (1) of the *differences* in rhetorical situations they encountered (or expected to encounter) in diverse genres, including academic writing, popular texts, and online or media-rich texts; (2) of what they liked *most* and *least* about each rhetorical situation; and (3) of what they would propose as a *set of guidelines* for good citizenship in each rhetorical situation. Use the lists for a whole-class discussion of the ways in which communication changes across forms of writing and what that means for academic expectations of students in college.

Design for Writing: Overview

> *Good visual design complements good writing; it does not replace it. Together writing and design are part of finding the best available means to communicate with readers.*
>
> –Susan Hilligoss

When addressing an audience, a speaker is judged visually and aurally. The speaker's appearance, tone of voice, and the degree to which he or she meets the audience's eyes all create an impression. Our rhetorical sense tells us that we ought to dress appropriately when we go before a committee to be interviewed for a scholarship. Classical rhetoricians called this aspect of our behavior *actio* or *pronunciatio*—delivery—and identified it as one of rhetoric's five arts or canons.

In classical rhetoric, *actio* referred exclusively to the delivery of a speech to an audience. In our literate culture, however, rhetoric must also include written communication, where the audience is removed from the writer's immediate proximity. The writer has a different set of cues than the speaker on which to rely to get his or her image across to the reader. Some primary cues, of course, must come from the writing itself: what it says, how it presents the writer's ideas and feelings, how it reflects him or her. But increasingly in this digital age, the visual rhetoric of documents is taking center stage. Thus, today, students *and* instructors need to pay special attention to the elements of design that add so much to the effectiveness of print documents.

For many instructors of writing, it has been all too easy to neglect *delivery*, which has long been cut out of the rhetorical tradition. Yet *actio* is of great importance to students' writing and may well become more so in the future. You should consider the importance of such issues to your own writing and share your thoughts with students. Also, you need to make very clear your requirements concerning visual rhetoric—perhaps even spelling them out in your syllabus.

Teaching Advice: Questions about Design

A great way to get students to appreciate the significance of the design choices of visual arguments is to ask them to manipulate selected images with standard computer programs such as Adobe Photoshop or Paintbrush. What happens when a picture of the human genome is juxtaposed over a baby? a sick patient? a field of identical tomatoes? an industrial smokestack? How does the color scheme affect the power of persuasion in the image? Ask students to explore black and white versus color, sepia versus primary colors. What audiences are addressed by different color schemes, font sizes, and visual tropes?

You might also ask students to write three paragraphs analyzing the effect of each visual manipulation. What have they learned from manipulating images about size, color, placement, font, and composition? Project several examples from the class on a large screen, and ask students to read their essays out loud to the class. Then spend some time getting feedback on both the images and essays from the class as a whole.

Teaching Advice: Document Design

It's crucial that students become aware of the entire package and presentation of their work, from the opening words to the overall format of their essays. You can help facilitate such attention by providing students with a "final checklist" to use in assessing their last revisions. Give students a handout or post questions on your course Web site. Delineate your precise expectations for document design, the way a paper will be formatted. It is also helpful to have a class dialogue about the different formatting expectations across disciplines and classes.

Teaching Advice: Planning a Visual Structure

To instruct students in the importance of planning a visual structure, you might inform them of the deep roots of visual design in classical rhetoric. In "*Actio:* A Rhetoric of Manuscripts," Robert Connors covers such document design concerns as "Type and Typefaces," "Paper," "Typography and Layout," and some "Minor Considerations." His overview ends with the following reminder regarding the powers—and limits—of planning any visual structure or document:

The rhetoric of manuscripts is a very small part of the entire rhetorical presentation of a writer. At its best, *actio* effaces itself and allows readers to concentrate on comprehension, aware only that the texts they hold are pleasant to the eye and to the touch. The most wonderful manuscript, however, cannot turn a poor piece of writing into a good one or make a vacuous essay meaningful. The best that the suggestions here can do is prevent a good piece of writing from being sabotaged by silly or careless physical presentation. Like speakers, who are scrutinized as soon as they walk out onto the platform, writers are being sized up as soon as their manuscripts fall from a manila envelope or are pulled from a pile. Attention to the tenets of *actio* can make certain that both writer and speaker are able to present their messages in the most effective way.

Paragraph breaks are also an element of *actio*. H. W. Fowler writes in *A Dictionary of Modern Usage*, "Paragraphing is also a matter of the eye. A reader will address himself more readily to his task if he sees from the start that he will have breathing-spaces from time to time than if what is before him looks like a marathon course." These principles are even more important in online documents, where space is at a premium. Ask students to remember *actio* when planning a visual structure or document.

Activity: Formatting

Ask students to work in small groups to share information about their approaches to formatting layout and design features for their texts. Working in groups of three or four, students should prepare a brief report for the class on "the top ten best layout and design features available." After the groups report, you can use the information they provide to discuss the aesthetics of document design, formatting, and visual rhetoric of the page. Get them thinking, along with you, about which design features are most appropriate—and which ones are inappropriate—for most of their college writing assignments.

Teaching Advice: Planning Visuals

In a 2000 issue of *College English*, Craig Stroupe argues that English studies "needs to decide not only whether to embrace the teaching of visual and information design in addition to verbal production, which some of the more marginalized elements of English Studies have already done, but, more fundamentally, whether to confront its customary cultural attitudes toward visual discourses and their insinuation into verbal texts." Similarly, teachers in writing classes need to confront the idea that visual images are subordinate to the verbal and that they serve as decoration to the true heart of the text that lies in its prose.

You can alert students to these preconceptions by asking them to take short articles from magazines, campus newspapers, and blogs and analyze how the texts function when paired with visual images. How do placement, color, size, and relationality affect the power of persuasion inherent in visual-verbal combinations? Have students draw up a brief list of "visual rhetoric" criteria on which to evaluate the design of texts containing images. Then ask them to experiment with manipulating the images: What happens when a different image is used in conjunction with a text? How does changing the visual structure produce a change in rhetorical meaning?

According to Brian Krebs, the Ninth Circuit Court of Appeals ruled in February 2002 that "while Web sites may legally reproduce and post 'thumbnail' versions of copyrighted photographs, displaying full-sized copies

of the images violates artists' exclusive right to display their own works."
At stake was a technological technique called "framing" or "inlinking" that imports images and displays them in full size in the new browser window. Such an appropriation of images is not considered "fair use" and thus violates copyright law. Let your students know about this new consequence of using technology to incorporate images in their writing, particularly if they cut and paste images from the Web.

Activity: Planning Visuals

As part of their next writing assignment, ask students to include a visual of some kind, labeled appropriately. Before allowing your students to hand in the final drafts of their papers, have them exchange these drafts for one final peer response, focusing purely on *actio*. In order to ensure that your students bring in a final typed draft, don't tell them ahead of time that these drafts will be reviewed. Provide each student with a pencil and eraser. Proofreading marks should be made in pencil lightly so that the author of the paper can erase them, if he or she chooses. It is important for students to realize that making or not making the suggested corrections is their choice. If a student finds substantial changes need to be made, then permit him or her to turn the paper in the next day.

Online Texts: Overview

Increasingly, for many of us, the basic document is a Web page or, less frequently, a CD-ROM—what I will call an e-document. . . . Now the challenge is to express [our] dynamic, multidimensional world in a virtual, multidimensional, and dynamic medium. Many of us now inhabit the new virtual world, but we still act and write as though we were permanent residents of Flatland.

–Lawrence M. Hinman

In his essay "Escaping from Flatland," Hinman goes on to say that the new dynamic, interactive, multimedia-filled Web page has led him to realize that "I no longer write as well as I used to. The medium has changed, and now I realize there are areas of writing in which I am less skilled." Like Hinman, most teachers of writing learned to write a text that was composed solely of words. The two last decades, however, have brought the changes Hinman talks about, and students are now quite comfortable with online and multimedia writing. While conventions to guide writers in these new forms are evolving, teachers need to become keen observers, taking note of features we find most effective in online texts and beginning the hard work of creating a pedagogy to encompass them.

At the same time, the development of Web texts should not be limited to student writers. In "Technology's Role in Creating the Shared-Learning Environment," Sheila Offman Gersh reminds us that we can dramatically revitalize and improve our pedagogy through rhetorically sound Web texts that engage and educate our student audience:

Teachers . . . can use the Internet to link their students to other classes to work collaboratively to further enrich any topic they are learning. This creates the "shared learning" environment around classroom instruction.

Teaching Advice: Planning an Online Text

As they plan their texts, ask students to consider rhetorical issues by filling out a brief form that can help them carry out an ongoing evaluation of their plan:

- audiences for my online text
- purpose of my text or site
- topic and title of my text or site
- the personality (or rhetorical stance) I want my text to have
- necessary content for my text (and why it is necessary)

Activity: Planning an Online Text

Ask students to work in pairs or groups of three to plan an online text in the format of a "storyboard" or graphic map. Tell them that such prewriting can be a great time-management technique. Suggest that they use index cards, one to represent the home page and another for each major page of the Web site that readers can access from the home page. For this early planning exercise, ask them to organize the Web site hierarchically—putting the home page at the top and then arranging the additional pages to follow. One goal of this exercise is to ask students to show the relationship of each page to the other pages. Finally, ask them to bring their storyboard plan to class for discussion and critical review.

Teaching Advice: Considering Types of Online Texts

In their book, *Web Style Guide: Basic Design Principles for Creating Web Sites*, Patrick Lynch and Sarah Horton talk extensively about "visual logic," showing how spatial organization of text and graphics on Web pages can "engage readers with graphic impact, direct their attention, prioritize the information they see, and make their interactions with your Web site more enjoyable and efficient." Students can profit from Lynch and Horton's advice by aiming to create a consistent and memorable visual hierarchy that emphasizes important elements and organizes the content in ways that are predictable to most readers. Getting real readers to respond to their site design is of great importance, since this kind of user feedback will help in revision of the design.

In *Digital Literacy*, Paul Gilster provides another perspective, commenting on the multimedia capabilities of hypertext:

> What is novel is the ability to connect everything from sound files to animation to moving video to textual documents within a single frame, a so-called page of information. We can do this because computers can digitize these forms of media; to a computer, a file is a file, so that we can connect to a movie clip with the same point-and-click techniques we use to access a text file. When we do this, we move beyond the bounds of pure hypertext into the realm of a far more facile beast called *hypermedia*. The underlying computer functions remain the same, but the kind of information we pull in with our browsers changes. For all practical purposes, in today's Web the terms *hypertext* and *hypermedia* have become synonymous, although we can always call upon the distinction between text and other forms of media when there is need to make a specific point.

Activity: Considering Types of Online Texts

Place each student with a buddy in order to collaborate on an analysis of the Web sites in the book. The buddy-team should take notes on the effectiveness of these pages and prepare a brief report for class. Remind students to include tips for how the pages could be improved.

Teaching Advice: Examining Features of Online Texts

In the October 1999 special issue of *Syllabus Web: Useful Information on Technology Used to Enhance Education*, the editors discuss the benefits of multimedia and digital content on the Web:

> Today's classrooms have come alive with dynamic animations, simulations, and visualizations that help illustrate complex concepts. Through multimedia, instructors can present material that might be difficult or impractical to bring to the lab or lecture hall. And with more advanced Web technologies, such as Java applications, back-end databases, and streaming media, multimedia content resources can be leveraged online to support campus-based courses or to reach distant learners.

Model the best rhetorical practices of using visuals and multimedia in your teaching. This will inspire students to incorporate dynamic technological visualizations in their own Web texts.

For example, Miriam Schacht, nervous about teaching in a computer-assisted classroom for the first time, asked her students to create multimedia autobiographical Web texts as part of their final writing projects. She used the assignment to model possibilities to the students and turned her "lack of expertise" to pedagogical advantage by modeling the learning process as well. The success of this experiment manifests itself on many levels, as seen in the student projects available through her online article's hypertext.

Paul Gilster does a fine job of alerting readers to the powerful rhetoric of hypertext, including its central paradox: "it establishes links to banks of information, leading to the assumption that ideas are always backed by evidence. [But] a hypertext discussion can be *manipulated* by the choice of those links. What appear to be inevitable connections to related facts are actually *choices* made by page designers whose views are reflected in their selection of links."

To help your students grasp this principle, ask them to go to a commercial Web site and study its links, reporting back to the class on what those links include, in what ways they are "slanted," and what links are obviously *not* included. Then, have them engage in the following activity.

Activity: Examining Features of Online Texts

Ask students to select two particularly effective and memorable Web sites to discuss in class. Then, working in groups of three, students should look for design principles that characterize the most effective home pages. Ask each group to present a report to the class based on its findings.

Activity: Thinking Critically about Argument in Online Texts

Building on students' familiarity with the Internet, ask them to work in small groups to identify three favorite Web sites. Each group should select two Web sites from the batch to present to the class. Perhaps one Web site is quite obviously an argument. But the second one may be a much more subtle form of persuasion. What is the Web site's message, pitch, or purpose? How does it sell something, convince the audience to believe something, or make a claim? Display the selected Web sites on a projector screen for the entire class to analyze. Let students present the major features of argument in each Web text. You might consider asking them to analyze popular social networking sites for arguments, as well. Are these arguments easy to identify? Are students aware of these arguments in their daily use of these sites or networks?

Teaching Advice: Putting Your Text Together

The online scholarly journal *Kairos* offers an entire host of assignments on writing online texts. Patricia Ventura, for example, in her essay for *Kairos*, asks students to translate a written essay into what she calls a "Websay." Her purpose is to have students "examine the ways in which Web writing both differs from and resembles traditional writing so that [students] will be able to produce Web projects that take full advantage of this medium." To do so successfully, students need to consider carefully the elements of visual design. Ventura emphasizes that they need to "transform"—not "transfer"—their documents for the Web. Experiment with a similar exercise in your class before assigning a more complex online writing project. Have students review their final Web texts and then revise and edit them as necessary.

Teaching Advice: Formal and Informal Electronic Communications

> With the development of the Internet, and . . . networked computers, we are in the middle of the most transforming technological event since the capture of fire.
>
> —John Perry Barlow

Now that students are raised in a computer-mediated environment, most of them see writing with computers as natural, even as easier than writing with pen and paper. Some students admit to learning to write on a keyboard, not by hand. This revolution is widespread across the United States, as most students have grown up with a relationship with computers that Cynthia Selfe calls indicative of "critical technological literacy." While discrepancies remain in underprivileged schools, neighborhoods, and families, and while some students take "oppositional" or "negotiated" stances toward technology, the majority of today's college students report what Barbara Duffelmeyer calls "comfortable oneness with technology." Knowing this can transform the way you implement writing with computers in your course and the way you teach formal and informal electronic writing.

As Chris M. Anson, a specialist in computers and composition, argues in a recent article: "Online communication with students is an idea that seems stale by now but is by no means fully exploited; only some teachers eagerly invite email from students, and only some students end up using it when invited."

Yet working with computers means making sure that you have access to proper and timely training in new technologies and support for your pedagogical innovations. Anson has argued in his assessment of national and institutional trends: "The quality of faculty interaction with students is a product of our *work*—our training, the material conditions at our institutions, how much support we get for developing our teaching and keeping up on research." Check with your institution's technology center or ask your chairperson for training workshops as part of your professional development.

Alice Trupe discusses how literacy has changed and highlights the emergence of writing as electronic communication in a *Kairos* article:

> The freshman essay and the research paper are vehicles through which students are expected to demonstrate their literacy. . . . Whereas these specialized genres for students have served as the measure of freshman writing ability for a hundred years, transformation of writing courses by computer technology is a recent phenomenon. Composition instructors first welcomed word processing because it facilitated production of the standard freshman essay. However, the move into electronic environments rapidly began to revolutionize classroom practices and genres. Today, the expanding possibilities for writing engendered through desktop publishing, email, Web-based bulletin boards, MOOs, Web page and other hypertext authoring, and presentation software show up the limitations the freshman essay imposes on thought and writing.

Trupe goes on to argue that despite our reliance on new technologies in the writing classroom, we still look to the essay as the "limiting genre that most of us expect first-year writers to master." Consequently, while "we may encourage them to explore the possibilities of interactive computer environments . . . in the final analysis, the test of what students have learned through classroom activities often remains the plain vanilla, five-paragraph essay, since that is what is assessed for a grade."

As teachers, however, we need to develop our own proficiency in teaching both formal and informal communication in online, technologically mediated environments. Our students will need to know so much more than how to write the "plain vanilla" five-paragraph essay.

Teaching Advice: Composing Academic and Professional Messages

In order to generate a discussion about best practices, ask students to respond to the following questions:

1. When you are writing on a computer, how often do you edit the subject line to reflect your purpose?

2. Do you consider various options for addressing your audience?

3. Do you show drafts of important electronic messages to friends or advisers?

4. When you write on a listserv or discussion forum, do you reread your message before posting? What words might be appropriate or inappropriate for an audience?

5. Do you use your spell checker to proof your messages and electronic postings?

You can use students' responses to these questions to lead a discussion on how to approach both formal and informal electronic communication.

Teaching Advice: Writing for Less Formal Situations

In order to establish the ground rules for informal electronic communication, review the guidelines in this section as a class. Then ask students to add to the list based on their own experience in order to construct a class etiquette list. Patrick Sullivan provides an excellent example of such a list of email etiquette in "Reimagining Class Discussion in the Age of the Internet" in *TETYC* 29.4 and urges teachers to "establish a strong online netiquette policy":

> Establishing such a policy is essential for creating a learning environment where students feel safe and comfortable enough to share their ideas and feelings. . . . It is important to establish ground rules about class discussion to ensure that conversations will not be confrontational, competitive, or unnecessarily argumentative. Some level of conflict is, of course, usually desirable in a class discussion, but teachers who hope to create a positive class environment online need to make it very clear that class discussions will also be collaborative in nature and collegial in tone.

In addition, you can ask students to analyze your own email style, tone, content, and use in order to generate class rules.

Activity: Writing for Less Formal Situations

Ask students to work in small groups to draw up a description of the ways in which electronic communication on social networking sites differs from more formal communications such as emails, letters, and the academic writing they do for most of their classes. You can use their small-group reports to generate a discussion about netiquette and about issues of style in different genres of writing.

Oral and Multimedia Presentations: Overview

> *Talking and eloquence are not the same: to speak, and to speak well, are two things.*
>
> —Ben Jonson

At the same time that oral discourse has been growing in importance in our culture, attention to orality has waned in college courses and in the college curriculum. This situation is, however, now being reversed, as many colleges and universities move to include attention to speaking and to oral presentations in their general education curriculum requirements. Students are being asked to give oral presentations in increasing numbers of classes, and they want and need help in responding to these demands.

New trends across the nation to incorporate multimedia presentations in the writing classroom also challenge us as teachers to reconsider what it is we are teaching in the first-year composition classroom. Remind students that "multimedia" does not mean PowerPoint alone. Overheads, posters, handouts, props, and dramatic enactments can all be part of a multimedia presentation. Often students translate "multimedia" as "technology" and don't realize that a powerful presentation can be produced using simply a poster, a carefully constructed handout, or voice and gesture alone. Encouraging students to work on oral and multimedia presentations will also help foster their development as writers in multiple media and hence help them begin to see connections between genres. As James Inman, Rachel Hallberg, and Courtney Thayer argue in "Disney Promotion Poster Analysis," we need to ask our students to "imagine new and important connections between technology-rich and non-technological genres of writing."

Indeed, the increasing affordability of programs like PowerPoint and Dreamweaver have highlighted the degree to which today's "writing" often combines media. But even before the Web, of course, what often appeared to be in one medium—a speech, let's say—was more accurately *multi*media: a televised speech and even a talk show host's monologue are delivered orally, but they have been previously written. And even the most traditional spoken lectures have long relied on illustrations that may include music, art, and other forms of media.

These possibilities of multimedia create special challenges for writing instructors who must learn how to discover, and then pass on to their students, the best advice about how to create multimedia presentations that are rhetorically effective.

Teaching Advice: Considering Assignment, Purpose, and Audience for Presentations

Before students get started on developing an oral or multimedia presentation, ask them to brainstorm about the assignment. Have them answer the following questions to get their ideas flowing:

- Who is the main audience? What would work best for this audience?
- What, above all, do you want your audience members to take away from the presentation?
- What are your strengths as a writer and a creative individual: public speaking? creative design? humor? clear explication?
- What do you want to learn from the process of creating a presentation? new skills in oral communication? effective ways of using PowerPoint? practice for poster sessions? presenting Webcasts?
- What should be most memorable in your presentation?
- What risks can you take?

Activity: Composing for Oral Presentations 1

In "Town Meetings," Gerry Brookes recommends asking students to prepare to speak very briefly (three minutes) on a topic of concern to them. In "town meeting" sessions that occur once a week, two or three students make their presentations. After each one, Brookes says, the class always applauds. Then the teacher poses a series of questions designed to "allow people to suggest alternative points of view, to offer supporting evidence, or to point out misjudgments of audience, without breaking into open disagreement." This kind of controlled response to the presentations, Brookes argues, allows students and instructor to help the speaker even when they disagree passionately about what she or he has said. Brookes recommends writing response notes to each speaker instead of giving formal grades, using the notes as the basis for conferences, and "giving a bit of extra credit if the spoken text is especially good." This class activity can help students learn the elements of an effective oral presentation within a collaborative and safe space.

Activity: Composing for Oral Presentations 2

To help students learn how to give effective oral presentations, ask students to prepare two-minute introductions of themselves near the beginning of the term (ideally on the second day of class). Put them into groups of three so that they will practice and present with two other colleagues. After the introductions of each group, use class time to talk about what elements were most effective in these presentations. Ask students to think about what was most memorable about these introductions, about what techniques seemed particularly successful, and about what was most threatening about this situation. Then ask the members of the group to comment on how the presentation changed with a little practice—what was improved and made better through time? As a follow-up exercise, ask students to write a journal entry about what lessons they could draw from the introductions about their own strengths and weaknesses as presenters.

Teaching Advice: Practicing Presentations

You may wish to ask students to evaluate one another's oral or multimedia presentations using an electronic peer-response form. Consider giving them a set of categories or a rubric to guide their responses. For example, you could ask that they make comments on strategy (adaptation to audience, opening and closing, visual aids); content (supporting materials and language, clarity, line of argument, anticipating and answering objections); organization (overview of main points, signposting, main points); and delivery (eye contact, conversational style, voice quality, gestures).

After each presentation, allow for five minutes of interactive questions and answers. Then ask students to write a short electronic commentary on the presentation and post it to your class's online course space. The benefits of asking students to provide their evaluative comments online are that the speaker can download and print all the comments at once, you avoid having to photocopy and assemble slips of feedback, and all class members can see what others have written and can learn from those peer responses how to rethink their own presentation strategies.

Activity: Practicing Presentations

Students will benefit greatly from working with one another to prepare and practice oral presentations. To help them get started on this work, group them in pairs or sets of three and allow them some class time to talk about their topics, to discuss their deadlines and time constraints, and to set up a schedule. Then ask them to meet outside class to hold group practice sessions. During these sessions, the listener(s) should take notes on three things: what they remember most vividly, what they don't understand, and what they need or want to hear more of. In order to encourage students to work seriously at these sessions, consider awarding some credit for this group work, and ask them to write individual summaries of what they did during practice sessions, how the practices helped them, and what might be done to improve future practice sessions.

Activity: Evaluating Presentations

Ask students to join two or more classmates and attend a presentation of interest to them, either on campus or in the larger community. All members of the group should take notes during the presentation on what they find effective and ineffective. Then the team should meet to compare notes and write up a brief collaborative review of the presentation and bring it to class for discussion.

Resources

Section	The St. Martin's Handbook	The Everyday Writer	EasyWriter
Visuals, Media, and Design	4j	9d	2f–2h
Thinking Critically about Visuals	7d	11b	3b
Working with Visuals	13e	17c	40b
Analyzing Visual Arguments	7d, 8e	11b, 12e	3b–3d
Organizing Visual Information	3e	7d	2d
Thinking about Genre	2e	5f	1f–1g
Questions about Design	7d	11b	3b
Document Design	4k	10a	2h–2i
Planning a Visual Structure	23a	4a	6a
Formatting	23b	4b	6b
Teaching Advice: Planning Visuals	23d	4d	6d

Planning an Online Text	21a1–21a2	2d	4b
Considering Types of Online Texts	21b–21c	2d	4b
Putting Your Text Together	21d	2d	4b
Considering Assignment, Purpose, and Audience for Presentations	22b	3b	4c
Composing for Oral Presentations	22c	3b	4c

Note: Depending on which book you are using, student essays may appear online rather than in print. Check the Directory of Student Writing for locations.

Writing in the Disciplines

Writing in Any Discipline: Overview

The belief that writing should be the concern of the entire school community underlies this chapter. According to Art Young and Toby Fulwiler, composition researchers and theorists such as James Britton, Janet Emig, James Kinneavy, James Moffett, Mina Shaughnessy, and Lillian Bridwell-Bowles have all variously suggested that student writing will not improve until students see writing at the center of their academic experience. They will learn to value it and practice it when it is incorporated usefully into the daily process of learning in all disciplines. Writing-across-the-curriculum programs work toward these goals. Over the last two decades, dozens of these programs have emerged in U.S. colleges and universities. Individual programs may differ in scope and practice, but all of them aim to improve student writing by encouraging faculty from across the disciplines to use writing regularly and thoughtfully in their classrooms.

Activity: Academic Work in Any Discipline

Have students pair up with a classmate or friend who intends to major in the same field. Then have the teams investigate the college Web site to locate two faculty members in that field and to learn about their scholarly work. One team member should contact a professor for an appointment to conduct an interview. (Make sure each group has a couple of backup professors on the list in case one is unavailable.) Before conducting their interview, remind students to review the information in this section to help them generate their questions. (See the cross-reference chart on page 162.) Each team should conduct the interview and write a brief summary of what the members have learned for the class.

Activity: Understanding Academic Assignments

If your students can provide assignments from various disciplines, have them do an analysis using the questions in the Analyzing an Assignment checklist in the book you are using. (See the cross-reference chart on page162.) Encourage them to work in groups to analyze the assignments and their expectations.

Activity: Learning Specialized Vocabulary

Ask students to work in groups of three. Each student should bring to class two copies of a short passage of approximately one hundred words taken from an article, an essay, or a textbook in a field with which he or she is familiar. Have students give a copy to each of their partners and ask them (1) to list terms, phrases, or concepts that seem to involve specialized or highly technical language, and (2) to define and explain these terms. Have students retrieve their articles and their partners' lists, check their efforts, and then, in discussion, clarify the terms for them. Discuss their confusion or lack of it.

This exercise gives students practice explaining basic terms in fields they are familiar with to a general audience. For example, the term *blastema* is basic knowledge to students in molecular genetics, as is *Cyrillic alphabet* to Slavic language majors. *Morpheme* is a basic concept to linguistics students, as is *hypotenuse* to geometry students. Thus, this exercise serves two purposes:

1. It helps students develop an awareness of how to adapt their language and explanations to audiences with different degrees of expertise or familiarity with a field's vocabulary.
2. It also allows students to test their own understanding of terms and concepts. One way we determine how well we understand concepts is to explain them to someone else.

For additional practice recognizing and using particular disciplinary language, divide the class into groups of no more than three students who are working in the same major field or in closely related fields. Have each group compile a glossary of twenty key terms that are essential to the field or fields. Ask students to alphabetize the terms and to define and explain each one.

Activity: Following Disciplinary Style

> There are many languages. There is the language of guns. There is the language of money. There is the language of human rights. There is the language of love.   —June Jordan

June Jordan might well have added to this quotation, "And there is a language of science, of law, of medicine." To get students thinking about the style of disciplines, ask them to write a journal entry about their experiences with writing in different disciplines. Some will have found writing difficult or easy regardless of the discipline, but others will have noted differences in the experiences, assignments, and teacher expectations associated with different subjects. These journal entries can be shared or simply written as preparation for an initial class discussion of disciplinary writing conventions.

Activity: Using Appropriate Evidence

In an intriguing letter to the editor, published in the *PMLA*, David Linton examines how scholarly contributors to a *PMLA* roundtable entitled "The Status of Evidence" use evidence themselves to make their claims. Ask your students to write similar letters to editors of journals that they read across various disciplines. In their letters, they should analyze and comment on the use of evidence in three of the journal's articles.

Writing for the Humanities: Overview

The central focus of the humanities is to explore, interpret, and reconstruct the human experience. To that end, we teach our students the disciplines of history, literature and literary analysis, drama, film, philosophy, and language. As you facilitate your students' learning in these disciplines, you might introduce your class to texts ranging from poems and plays to novels, articles, philosophical treatises, films, and translations.

Teaching Advice: Writing Texts in the Humanities

Ask students to read Bonnie Sillay's student essay in this chapter, noting where the writer uses material from literary texts—examples, quotations, and so on—to support her thesis. Point out the critical role that such textual evidence plays in any essay whose writer adopts a text-based stance. Have students emulate this use of evidence in their own essays.

Activity: Writing Texts in the Humanities 1

Ask students to choose an inspiring film, literary work, or painting and to write a short essay explaining to their peers how the work affects them. Next, have students exchange essays for peer review, reminding the reviewers to focus on how the essay's content and how learning about the writer's relationship to the work reveals the power of strong writing to move and persuade.

Activity: Writing Texts in the Humanities 2

Ask students to work with a partner. Ask for two students to volunteer their papers to be used as models and have half the teams analyze one paper and half analyze the other, using the principles and guidelines presented throughout this chapter. Each team should write a two- or three-paragraph peer response to the student essay and bring it to class for discussion. Do both essays succeed in the same way, or do they have different strengths given their purposes?

Writing for the Social Sciences: Overview

In an article for *College English*, Peter Elbow compares his experiences as both a composition teacher and a teacher of literature. What characterizes composition for him is its focus on useful instruction:

> When I finally came to see myself as a composition person, I felt an enormous relief at finally feeling *useful*—as though I could make an actual difference for people. I'd never felt solidly useful trying to teach and write about literature. I'm proud that composition is the only discipline I know, outside of schools of education, where members feel their field has a built-in relationship to teaching and to students.

The idea of writing instruction as inherently useful—related to purpose and student goals—is nowhere more appropriate than in composition classes, where we may need to teach students to write for the social sciences. Indeed, many students in our first-year classes go on to major in such fields as psychology, economics, anthropology, political science, and sociology. We can help prepare them for their future majors and careers through a focus on writing as a process of discovering knowledge in a particular field, for a particular audience. The same rhetorical foundations that students need to write a compelling public-policy analysis will help them craft a careful psychological study. At the same time, we can best serve our students by fostering their spirit of inquiry, showing them how to seek out the resources they need to pursue their own research interests, and leading them toward viewing writing as a critical means of communicating across all disciplines.

Teaching Advice: Reading Texts in the Social Sciences

If your composition course includes social science readings, you may find it difficult to tell how comprehensively students can process the material. One solution, suggested by Joe Law in *Writing across the Curriculum*, is to design weekly quizzes for students to complete on a computer during class or through a course Web site. Law also has students log their reading, research, and field-observation notes through technological means so that he can respond quickly to each student's work.

Teaching Advice: Writing Texts in the Social Sciences

One way for students to master material in the social sciences is through writing assignments that engage their critical and imaginative skills. In "Writing to Learn History," Donald Holsinger advocates using a variety of writing projects to engage students in the subject matter: course journals, simple writing exercises as preparation for in-class discussions, and detailed response papers that challenge students to write about specific statements and questions rather than vague topics. In addition, Holsinger suggests, giving students opportunities to write frequently and freely helps them become strong writers of texts in the social sciences. You might assign larger projects in developmental steps so that students work through the stages of writing. Have students revise and resubmit their work as if it were being submitted to a journal in the field. Finally, have students write to different audiences and from different perspectives.

Activity: Writing Texts in the Social Sciences 1

You might get students started on creative and engaging writing projects by asking them to examine various models of scholarly writing in the social sciences. Divide the class into groups of three, and send them to the library to find several journal articles from different publications in a particular field (psychology, anthropology, political science, sociology, economics, or education, for example). Ask each group to perform a rhetorical analysis of the writing in the articles, assessing it for discipline-specific terminology, construction of knowledge (quantitative or qualitative), supporting evidence, and formal properties (organization, voice, and subsections). Then ask each group to compose a "mock" article to be published in one of the journals. Have them model their text on one of the examples and then write a brief reflection about what they have learned from this "pedagogy of models."

Activity: Writing Texts in the Social Sciences 2

Your students may feel hesitant to express their own individuality in their writing for the social sciences. You might initiate a class discussion on what it means to write with an objective voice versus writing with the strategic use of ethos. Analyze Katie Paarlberg's psychology report in the book for its uniqueness of style. Ask students to write a short response to the report, commenting on the appropriateness of Katie's choices for her particular academic audience.

Writing for the Natural and Applied Sciences: Overview

Jacques Cousteau once wrote, "What is a scientist after all? It is a curious man looking through a keyhole, the keyhole of nature, trying to know what's going on." Many of the students in your writing classes will go on to pursue scientific majors and careers. But remember that curiosity—the spirit of inquiry that drives research—is crucial to successful writing for any purpose. Teaching students to recognize and cultivate their own spirit of inquiry will help make them more effective writers in your composition classes and in their future professions.

Teaching Advice: Reading Texts in the Natural and Applied Sciences

The famous physicist Robert Millikan wrote that being a strong reader—having what he called the "habit of attention"—is crucial to academic success: "Cultivate the habit of attention and try to gain opportunities to hear wise men and women talk. Indifference and inattention are the two most dangerous monsters that you'll ever meet. Interest and attention will insure to you an education." To help familiarize students with the conventions of science writing, have them peruse online journals in several different scientific fields available through your library's database collection and conduct a detailed analysis of the differences in the way each field organizes information. How do journals for professionals in a given field present information? How does this differ from articles meant for a more general audience? You might also have students explore how different journals in one field of scientific study differ from one another. Ask students to write a brief report on their findings.

Activity: Reading Texts in the Natural and Applied Sciences

The connection between facts and claims in the sciences, as in all subject areas, is created by the author rather than simply revealed by the data. So students should read both facts and claims with a questioning eye: Did the scientist choose the best method to test the hypothesis? Are there other reasonable interpretations of the experiment's results? Do other studies contradict the conclusions of this experiment? When you read specialized texts in the sciences with questions like these in mind, you are reading—and thinking—like a scientist.

Ask students to share their responses to these questions. Then have them interview science professors to obtain professional responses to the same questions. Ask students to record the professors' comments and bring a transcript of the interviews to class. Begin a dialogue in class about the rhetorical purpose of the use of composition elements in the natural and applied sciences. If students understand the reasons for following particular writing guidelines, they will be more prone to follow them and to invest time in writing well within the discipline.

Activity: Writing Texts in the Natural and Applied Sciences

Have students work in peer-review groups on their literature reviews, research reports, and lab reports. You can get them started by modeling a peer review of Allyson Goldberg's lab report in this section. Ask students to suggest textual revisions, alternatives in format and presentation, and an alternate introduction. As a class, make the changes collaboratively, using the board or an overhead projector. Be sure to emphasize to students the point made in this chapter—that most scientific writing is collaborative.

Writing for Business: Overview

All professional activities require strong and persuasive writing as well as adherence to the formal conventions of a particular audience. Companies and business organizations look for solid, well-written, and carefully constructed cover letters and résumés that attend to the rhetorical situation. Grants and business proposals can be highly successful if attention is given to the writing process for each of these important genres. As writing teachers, we often find that our students need advice and instruction in writing for business situations. You can help them develop business-writing strategies by leading them through the sections in the book on becoming strong readers and writers of texts in business.

Teaching Advice: Reading Texts for Business

In a study of strong business writing, Lee Odell and Dixie Goswami examined writing done by administrators and caseworkers. By interviewing the study participants and analyzing the writing samples they collected, the authors found that while workers in different positions write differently and justify their writing choices differently, all writers are sensitive to rhetorical context. Their writing varied according to its type, audience, and subject. Nevertheless, what the study participants termed "acceptable writing" remained constant across different positions.

Conduct a version of this study with your class. Ask students to bring in articles from business magazines, memos and reports from print and online sources, and other examples of business writing. During a class discussion about the rhetorical context for each piece of writing, compile a list on the board of the shared qualities of "acceptable writing" among the different types of business writing.

Activity: Reading Texts for Business

Have students work in groups of two or three to analyze the Abbott and Abernathy memo, using advice in this section. Students should note the memo's strengths and weaknesses, jot down any topics they think the memo overlooks, and mark any spots where they think information can be deleted. The groups should be prepared to explain their choices. Review the results of their analyses in a class discussion.

Activity: Writing Texts for Business

Keeping Odell and Goswami's findings in mind, as well as the class-generated list detailing the qualities of "acceptable writing," ask students to compose their own collaborative piece of writing in emulation of one of the models they selected in the preceding activity. Have each group take on a different type of writing—memos, email messages, letters, or résumés. Then discuss the similarities and differences among the various texts and how the qualities of each text are determined by its rhetorical situation.

Activity: Writing Memos

Ask students to work in groups of three or four to write a memo about the course—the activities, the instructor's expectations, and the like—for students who will be enrolled in the course next term. Then, to encourage students' consideration of audience, have them write different versions of the memo to friends, teachers, and so on. This activity will provide practice in a genre that is unfamiliar to many students.

Activity: Writing Résumés

Because employers spend so little time reading résumés, the format, the design, and just plain good writing are especially critical. For this exercise, ask students to bring in drafts of their résumés. Have them work in groups of two or three to review each résumé and offer suggestions based on their reading of this section. In addition, you may want students to review the principles of document design. If you are teaching in a technology-enhanced classroom, have students work with electronic versions of their résumés, revising the documents to incorporate the peer-review suggestions. Project examples on a screen, and discuss with the class the difference that small changes can make, paying particular attention to audience.

Resources

Section	The St. Martin's Handbook	The Everyday Writer	EasyWriter
Academic Work in Any Discipline	59	60	5
Understanding Academic Assignments	59c	60b	5a
Learning Specialized Vocabulary	59d	60c	5a
Following Disciplinary Style	59e	60d	5a
Using Appropriate Evidence	59f	60e	5a
Writing Texts in the Humanities	60b	61b	5b
Reading Texts in the Social Sciences	61a	62a	5c
Writing Texts in the Social Sciences	61b	62b	5c
Reading Texts in the Natural and Applied Sciences	62b	63b	5d
Writing Texts in the Natural and Applied Sciences	62c	63c	5d
Reading Texts for Business	63a	64a	5e
Writing Texts for Business	63b	64b	5e

Note: Depending on which book you are using, student essays may appear online rather than in print. Check the Directory of Student Writing for locations.

Writing for the Public

Overview

Regardless of their majors, your students will certainly be writing for some kind of public—and most are already doing so. Ask them whether they agree that good writing should "make something happen in the world," as Andrea Lunsford's longitudinal study of Stanford students argued. If so, what would they like to see their writing accomplish? (If not, what do they think writing should do?) You may want to begin the discussion by asking students to define "public writing." Is any writing today truly "private"? You can point out that any effective writing tries to get readers to do or feel something.

The focus of the chapter(s) is on public writing that tries to get its audience to take some action in the community. Ask students to analyze the community and the action desired for the examples given in the book. You may also want to bring in examples of writing that have inspired or moved people to effective action (and be prepared to talk about public discourse that may move people to actions the writer may not have intended, such as a fiery speech that resulted in violence or rioting). Walk your students through the rhetorical approach, language, and design of several pieces of public writing and ask them to analyze the intended audience, the goal of the writing, and whether they think the writing would have the desired effect.

Activity: Identifying Your Audience

Ask your students to think of public writing that they have done (some may need prompting, but remind them that online writing for friends or for a course blog also count). Have them bring in an example of something they've written that was meant to be seen by an audience and ask each writer to write a short analysis of the audience and purpose he or she had in mind and the response to the piece: Who was the writer trying to reach? Why did he or she choose a particular medium or genre? Did the piece successfully reach the desired audience? What response did it receive? How could the piece have been more successful in achieving the writer's goals?

Activity: Connecting with Your Audience

Ask students to work in groups of three or four to collect examples of public writing in various genres and media—such as a protest sign or an event flyer. Have them choose one, and then draft up a brief explanation of the intended audience. Have them analyze the creator's use of medium, timing, and language. Is the purpose clear, and does it successfully appeal to the desired audience? Is this example of public writing in the social realm effective? Why, or why not?

Resources

Section	The St. Martin's Handbook	The Everyday Writer	EasyWriter
Writing for the Public	66	19, 20	29, 30
Identifying Your Audience	66a	19, 20	29, 30
Connecting with Your Audience	66b	19, 20	29, 30

Note: Depending on which book you are using, student essays may appear online rather than in print. Check the Directory of Student Writing for locations.

Helping Multilingual Writers

Writing in U.S. Academic Contexts: Overview

Within the many strands of U.S. culture are countless multilingual students who encounter American academic conventions as confusing restrictions on the ways of reading, writing, and thinking that they have practiced for so long. Whether we consider these U.S. conventions in terms of "contrastive rhetorics" or "second-language issues," we need to be sensitive to the fact that U.S. academic conventions comprise a culture with a discourse and philosophy that can intimidate many multilingual students.

If the assumption "we all know good writing when we see it" governs our approach to teaching composition, how will we incorporate a concern for multilingual writers whose ways of engaging texts, assuming expectations for readers and writers, and personal or academic voices may not conform to such models? The notes provided here can begin to suggest alternative ways of approaching the teaching of writing to multilingual students.

Teaching Advice: Meeting Expectations for U.S. Academic Writing

While the "process movement" has been all the rage in composition studies, Ilona Leki tells us that ESL teaching has only recently shifted from structure-based language instruction to process-based instruction. In order to achieve the task of teaching students how to produce effective academic writing, you will need to engage your multilingual students using a process model, not a transmission model of writing pedagogy.

Share with your students Min-Zhan Lu's moving personal essay, "From Silence to Words: Writing as Struggle" (available in Sondra Perl's collection *Landmark Essays on Writing Process*), and have them discuss Lu's writing process. What academic styles did she encounter on her journey? What academic genres have your students encountered? What counts as "standard" in their home countries? When did they make their second (or third) language acquisition? You might also share with students stories about famous novelists who chose to write in second languages, such as Joseph Conrad and Samuel Beckett. How did these writers master the particular style or genre of a given audience and make their living by it? What can your students learn from such tales? How have cultures and expectations for assimilation changed since Conrad and Beckett? How are they different in the United States versus England, Mexico, or Japan?

You might use this discussion as a segue into the following activity, which treats some of the specific difficulties students may have with genre conventions.

Activity: Understanding Genre Conventions

Ilona Leki advocates immersion in language, especially reading, as vital for developing writing skills and understanding genre conventions. In her book *Understanding ESL Writers*, Leki recommends classroom practices, analyzes student writing, and surveys findings of contrastive rhetoric for several cultures. Similarly, Vivian Zamel, in "Writing One's Way into Reading," argues that reading and writing are interactive, mutually beneficial tasks.

Building off this research, have students in your classes share the responses they produced for the genre features. How do native speakers approach and analyze a text's genre features in contrast to multilingual speakers? What genres seem most and least familiar to readers of certain cultures? This box can be found in section 54b of *The St. Martin's Handbook*, section 55c of *The Everyday Writer*, and section 33b of *EasyWriter*.

Teaching Advice: Adapting Structures and Phrases from a Genre

Sandra Cisneros tells her readers to "write about what makes you different." Indeed, if your students are multilingual writers, then their own experiences form a veritable treasure trove of material for academic, professional, and personal essays. Encourage your students to write from what they know but also to begin to look for models of writing in the academic texts they will encounter through their reading. Have them avoid possible plagiarism by working through the appropriate section of their book.

Teaching Advice: Strategies for Learning from Search Engines

In her 1997 address to the Conference on College Composition and Communication, Cynthia Selfe discussed contemporary expectations for texts in a technological age:

> Technological literacy—meaning computer skills and the ability to use computers and other technology to improve learning, productivity and performance—has become as fundamental to a person's ability to navigate through society as traditional skills like reading, writing and arithmetic.

In *Literacy and Computers*, Cynthia Selfe and Susan Hilligoss expand further on the significance of technologically mediated texts for U.S. academic conventions:

> Technology, along with the issues that surround its use in reading- and writing-intensive classrooms, both physically and intellectually disrupts the ways in which we make meaning—the ways in which we communicate. Computers change the ways in which we read, construct, and interpret texts. In doing so, technology forces us to rethink what it means to be human. We need more problems like this.

Share the preceding passages with your students. Do they agree that technology has transformed writing and ways of making meaning through language and genres? How does America's access to computers change the way writers communicate across the globe? How do students from other countries and cultures respond to new technological environments? What can be learned from search engines about the structure of language in U.S. contexts and the ever-changing American vernacular? How might such technologies facilitate or hinder language acquisition and usage? After this discussion, you might engage students with the following activity.

Activity: Strategies for Learning from Search Engines

Give students the following quotation to analyze. You might post it for the class through an electronic discussion board.

> The last time somebody said, "I find I can write much better with a word processor," I replied, "They used to say the same thing about drugs." —Roy Blount Jr.

Ask students to write a brief response—to be posted to the discussion board—about the specific words, phrases, and expressions used in the passage. Then have them comment on the textual and cultural allusions inherent in the passage, and ask them to create a thesis about the way in which the language conveys the main idea of the passage. To further the dialogue, ask each student to respond to one other student's post. Choose a few postings from the class to generate discussion on how writing in the United States reflects a dependence on technology, genres, and cultural contexts.

Clauses and Sentences

One difficultly that teachers of multilingual writers encounter is the fact that the requirements for forming sentences differs from language to language, so the rules of English may not seem intuitive to some students. The two following exercises aim to help students develop a stronger grasp of English sentences and clauses by developing their ability to correctly take dictation.

Activity: Clauses and Sentences 1

In "Dictation as a Measure of Communicative Competence," Sandra Savignon argues that a student's success in taking dictation is a strong indicator of that student's language proficiency, for that student is *hearing* the language correctly. You might use the following passage for this kind of exercise:

> In prerevolutionary Cambodian society, whether a family belonged to the upper class or the peasantry, and whether they were ethnic Cambodian, or of Chinese or Vietnamese origin, the mother dealt with all household matters, child rearing in particular, and the prosperity, well-being, and reputation of the household depended mostly on her. The father dealt with the outside world and provided major family support. Because social norms based on Buddhist teachings promoted male-female equality, many women engaged in business ventures. When necessary, children helped their mothers to earn extra income, and there was usually a strong empathy between mothers and children. Even after children married and set up their own nuclear households, they continued to interact closely with their parents and siblings for mutual physical, emotional, and financial needs.
> The legal and cultural norm of duty to family members based on Buddhist precepts covered such things as parental authority, arrangement of proper marriages for children, provision

of support in the event of divorce and in old age, inheritance, adoption, guardianship, and provision of proper funeral arrangements.

Children generally received a great deal of affection in the first years of life not only from parents, but also from other adults and adolescents. But as they grew, older children were expected to conform to norms of politeness and obedience.

Although some competition was present in games, the stress was on playing rather than winning. . . .

By age 10 or so, both sexes had been taught basic skills necessary to be useful members of society. Boys, particularly in villages, learned agricultural techniques, while girls learned household duties. In adolescent years, the two sexes were segregated in school, which was strictly a place for education, and not for entertainment or romance. Premarital sex was deplored and sexual knowledge not considered suitable for children because it was considered to lead to desire and trouble. Adults also did not display physical love publicly even after marriage. Ideally, marriages were arranged by parents.

–Usha Welaratna, "A Khmer Perspective"

You may also ask your students to read aloud their dictations, taking care to notice whether, as they read aloud, they correct any of the mistakes they've made in their transcriptions.

Activity: Clauses and Sentences 2

Read aloud to the class the following passage from Amy Tan's "The Language of Discretion," and then ask students to list her allegations. After you have written their lists of allegations on the board, ask students to respond to Tan's argument, providing examples from their own language when possible.

Having listened to both Chinese and English, I . . . tend to be suspicious of any comparisons between the two languages. Typically, one language—that of the person doing the comparing—is often used as the standard, the benchmark for a logical form of expression. And so the language being compared is always in danger of being judged deficient or superfluous, simplistic or unnecessarily complex, melodious or cacophonous. English speakers point out that Chinese is extremely difficult because it relies on variations in tone barely discernible to the human ear. By the same token, Chinese speakers tell me English is extremely difficult because it is inconsistent, a language of too many broken rules, of Mickey Mice and Donald Ducks.

Even more dangerous to my mind is the temptation to compare both language and behavior *in translation*. To listen to my mother speak English, one might think she has no concept of past or future tense, that she doesn't see the difference between singular and plural, that she is gender blind because she calls my husband "she." If one were not careful, one might also generalize that, based on the way my mother talks, all Chinese people take a circumlocutory route to get to the point. It is, in fact, my mother's idiosyncratic behavior to ramble a bit.

–Amy Tan, "The Language of Discretion"

Nouns and Noun Phrases: Overview

Assessment of student writing is already a complex field of study, and the assessment of ESL student writing can be even trickier, especially when the teacher doesn't feel prepared to teach or evaluate ESL students.

But in "Assessment of ESL Students in Mainstream College Composition," Lisa Hillenbrand addresses the major concerns of writing instructors by speaking to issues of "Unraveling the Rhetoric," "Moving Away from the Error Obsession," and "Methods of Marking and Evaluating." She offers several substantive practices for classroom instructors.

The following activities should be helpful in giving students extra practice on the particularly thorny issues of count and noncount nouns and definite and indefinite articles.

Activity: Using Count and Noncount Nouns

As you talk with your class about count and noncount nouns, you will have to discuss the redundancies of the English language. Ask your students to bring in an essay they're working on and to write out the first paragraph, giving themselves plenty of space to mark out the redundancies of their English prose, particularly as redundancy does or does not apply to instances involving count and noncount nouns.

Activity: Using Articles

Ask students to copy out a passage from an in-progress essay and label as definite or indefinite the articles they use. Students should be able to explain their choice of article in each case. When students use nouns *without articles*, they should also be able to explain their syntactical decision.

Activity: Using Nouns in Specific Languages

Break the class into groups, and make a list of the distinguishing characteristics among *nouns* in each group member's primary language. Have students work together to prepare a lesson about these characteristics to present to the other groups. When they take the time to see and hear their native languages through the eyes and ears of a nonnative speaker, students will be better able to teach their own languages as well as to become more adept at learning the nuances of other languages—in this case, standard academic English.

Verbs and Verb Phrases: Overview

In "The Poetry of ESL Error," Melissa Allen discusses her evolution from an error-oriented, frustrated ESL instructor to a relaxed, fascinated instructor of ESL students. She writes that she began enjoying her teaching and her students when she realized that they were telling her things she didn't know; they were provoking her to think. "[T]hey were using the English language in interesting ways, with nuance and subtlety, with fascinating sounds and rhythms and silences. Even the errors sometimes had a certain something—poetry?"

Allen's realization changed her attitude about the goal of ESL teaching, and she argues that to concentrate on making ESL students write like native speakers is to "deprive them, ourselves, and our language of much that is enriching about the way ESL students use English." Hers is a compelling argument, which is most convincing in the list of "error-free" ESL sentences she includes. She describes these sentences as having "a nonnative flavor":

1. I went outside and smoked down my anger.
2. I cheered him on his success.
3. I looked through the list of names, but my name didn't come out for me.
4. When I feel oppressed in the chest, I like to listen to rock music.
5. I imagined she was a ferocious person who had timid ideas.
6. Your brain wants to eat more air than you are giving it.

7. Our music filled the room with warm heart.

8. It is useless to continue this barren argument.

You might share some of these sentences with your class, which would prepare them for the following activity.

Activity: Verbs and Verb Phrases

Ask for volunteers to share their "poetic" and other nonnative uses of English. If your students are working in groups, a native speaker of English might be able to locate such impressive examples of English usage.

Prepositions and Prepositional Phrases: Overview

Sandra Savignon, pioneer in communicative competence, is credited with influencing second-language teaching worldwide. Her work focuses on theoretical and research bases for language teaching, curriculum design, and testing procedures that encourage the learner to combine rule-based knowledge of several areas in order to negotiate meaning in a second language. In *Communicative Competence: Theory and Classroom Practice*, the phrase "communicative competence" includes "knowledge of sociolinguistic rules, or the appropriateness of an utterance in addition to knowledge of grammar rules." As she notes, "the development of the learners' communicative abilities is seen to depend not so much on the time they spend rehearsing grammatical patterns as on the opportunities they are given to interpret, to express, and to negotiate meaning in real life situations."

The following activity should help you give students some extra practice working to improve their grasp of how to use prepositions idiomatically.

Activity: Using Prepositions Idiomatically

Ask your students to break into groups and discuss their language backgrounds. First, consider an American attitude that all people should either know or learn English. What is their response? Second, they may want to consider the idea that everyone—including those smug Americans—should learn at least one foreign language. What are the advantages of knowing another language? another culture? Finally, ask students to focus on any prepositions and prepositional phrases they have used in this discussion, noting those that seem problematic. Use these examples for class discussion.

Resources

Section	The St. Martin's Handbook	The Everyday Writer	EasyWriter
Meeting Expectations for U.S. Academic Writing	54a	55–55a	33–33a
Understanding Genre Conventions	54b	55b–55c	33a–33b
Adapting Structures and Phrases from a Genre	54c	55c	33b
Strategies for Learning from Search Engines	54d	55d	33c
Clauses and Sentences	55	56	34
Nouns and Noun Phrases	56	57	35
Using Articles	56d	57e	35c
Verbs and Verb Phrases	57	58	36
Prepositions and Prepositional Phrases	58	59	37

Note: Depending on which book you are using, student essays may appear online rather than in print. Check the Directory of Student Writing for locations.